Journal of
MEDIA ECONOMICS

Volume 17, Number 2   2004

SPECIAL ISSUE ON DIVERSITY AND DIVERSIFICATION
Guest Editor: John Dimmick

CONTRIBUTORS

John Dimmick is an associate professor in the School of Communications, The Ohio State University, 154 N. Oval Mall, Columbus, OH 43210.

Mara Einstein is an assistant professor of media studies at Queens College, City University of New York, 65–30 Kissena Blvd., Flushing, NY 11367.

John Hagedoorn is an associate professor of economics and business administration, Department of Organization and Strategy, University of Maastrict, P.O. Box 616, Maastrict, The Netherlands 6200 MD.

Shu-Fang Lin is a PhD student in the School of Communications, The Ohio State University, 154 N. Oval Mall, Columbus, OH 43210.

Daniel G. McDonald is a professor in the School of Communications, The Ohio State University, 154 N. Oval Mall, Columbus, OH 43210.

François Moreau is an associate professor in the Laboratoire d'Econométrie, Conservatoire National des Arts et Métiers, 2 Rue Conté, Paris, France 75003.

Stéphanie Peltier is an associate professor in the Departement Techniques de Commercialisation, 14 Rue Francois de Vaux de Foletier, La Rochelle Cedex 01, France 17026.

Jacqueline Pennings is on the faculty of economics and business administration, Department of Organization and Strategy, University of Maastrict, P.O. Box 616, Maastrict, The Netherlands 6200 MD.

Hans van Kranenburg is on the faculty of economics and business administration, Department of Organization and Strategy, University of Maastrict, P.O. Box 616, Maastrict, The Netherlands 6200 MD.

INTRODUCTION

John Dimmick
School of Communications
The Ohio State University

This issue of the *Journal of Media Economics* deals with diversity and diversification. Although they have been treated as separate constructs, they are in fact mathematically identical. Both constructs, as McDonald and Dimmick (2003) point out, are exemplars of what Junge (1994) called dual-concept diversity.

As identical constructs they can be indexed by the same measures such as some version of the Simpson (1949) index or the information theory measure. All of the contributors to this issue use one or the other of these indexes to measure diversity or diversification.

Diversity, especially in broadcast programming, has played a major role in policy discussions on both sides of the Atlantic. The reason for the importance of the construct, however, is not often made explicit. Diversity in media content is important because the greater the variety or breadth of media content the greater the probability that media consumers can obtain utility or gratification from that content. Conversely, low diversity in media content means that consumers encounter fewer opportunities to obtain utility or gratification. Hence, consumer welfare is served by greater rather than lesser diversity.

Diversification, whether it is conceptualized as the variety of businesses in which a media firm engages, the diversity of its product offerings, or the range of geographic regions in which a media firm does business, is important for three reasons. First, a firm that is engaged in a number of enterprises is less vulnerable to disastrous environmental changes that affect one of its markets. Second, the diversified firm can achieve efficiencies through economies of scope, which its single enterprise counterparts cannot accomplish. Third, the multiple enterprise firm can engage in cross-subsidies to maintain a start-up business until it is profitable or to sustain a business that is temporarily experiencing a downturn in its economic fortunes.

Requests for reprints should be sent to John Dimmick, School of Communication, The Ohio State University, 154 N. Oval Mall, Columbus, OH 43210. E-mail: dimmick.1@osu.edu

The articles in this issue are suitably diverse in the media industries on which they focus and in the countries represented by their authors. Van Kranenburg, Hagedoorn, and Pennings take the publishing industry as their subject, whereas Moreau and Peltier have researched the film industry. Einstein and McDonald and Lin report findings on diversity in the U.S. television industry, albeit in different time periods.

Diversity and diversification may be related in ways beyond their mathematical structure. The long-term trends in media industries toward corporate diversification through acquisition and merger and the globalization of media markets raise questions concerning the impact of the diversification of media firms upon the content diversity of media in both domestic and international markets. Such questions provide a potentially fruitful area of investigation for future studies in media economics.

REFERENCES

Junge, K. (1994). Diversity of ideas about diversity measurement. *Scandinavian Journal of Psychology, 36,* 16–26.

McDonald, D., & Dimmick, J. (2003). The conceptualization and measurement of diversity. *Communication Research, 30*(1), 60–79.

Simpson, E. H. (1949). Measurement of diversity. *Nature, 163,* 688.

Measurement of International and Product Diversification in the Publishing Industry

Hans van Kranenburg, John Hagedoorn, and
Jacqueline Pennings
Department of Organization and Strategy
Faculty of Economics and Business Administration
University of Maastricht, The Netherlands

Corporate diversification has become an integral part of the strategy of many publishing companies. These diversification strategies may include both product diversification and international geographic diversification. This study demonstrates the diversification strategy of large-sized publishing companies. A number of measures and techniques are used to measure the diversification of these companies. We construct an additional measure to show the international diversification of the publishing companies. The findings indicate the existence of a set of common underlying dimensions or factors between a few measures, although no evidence of unidimensionality amongst all diversification measures exists. The various diversification indicators measure different aspects of diversification of publishing companies. Our data show that the publishing companies diversify into related activities and businesses and that, in particular, North American publishing companies do not diversify internationally.

Corporate diversification has become an integral part of the strategy of many publishing companies. These diversification strategies may include both product diversification and international geographic diversification. Nowadays, the information and communications landscape is a playing field much larger than the traditional publishing sector, and many companies have to redefine their "core" businesses. In particular, the use of new information and communication technologies has introduced a new phase in the evolution of the traditional media industry.

Requests for reprints should be sent to Hans van Kranenburg, Department of Organization and Strategy, Faculty of Economics and Business Administration, University of Maastricht, P.O. Box 616, 6200 MD Maastricht, The Netherlands. E-mail: h.vankranenburg@OS.unimaas.nl

New technologies such as the Internet make it possible to combine traditional and new businesses with an additional element that was missing in the earlier markets: interactivity. In other words, publishing is now part of the global information and communications industries and interacts with many different fields within this group of industries and technologies.

Due to trends in business globalization, convergence of different information and communications markets, technological and demographical developments, and the economic need for an increasing critical mass, companies have adapted to these changes and responded quickly to create or to sustain their competitive advantages. The wave of mergers and acquisitions in the media landscape during the 1990s is an indication of the popularity of diversification as a viable corporate strategy for publishing companies. Companies have expanded horizontally, vertically, and globally to maximize their competitive advantages and to strengthen their product portfolio. The leading companies in this area have indeed preferred to diversify into a number of unrelated businesses and related businesses that are centered on their traditional core business (Kranenburg, Cloodt, & Hagedoorn, 2001). In general, these companies have followed a strategy of gradual diversification into related new businesses. In addition, the strategy of these companies has changed toward a focus of expansion in foreign markets. An important element is found in the preference for the location of acquired companies in specific regions. For instance, European companies are becoming more focused on acquiring specialized North American companies that have a competitive advantage in state-of-the-art technologies (Bennett, 1999).

The purpose of this article is to establish a better understanding of the diversification strategy of companies operating in a media industry, considering the various developed measures on diversification. In the industrial organization and management literature, many measures are developed to demonstrate the diversification level of companies. The majority of measures are focused on product diversification (Jacquemin & Berry, 1979; Kim, 1989; Rumelt, 1974; Varadarajan & Ramanujam, 1987). However, empirical evidence shows that many leading media companies are expanding internationally to exploit emerging opportunities for international business, by finding new markets and additional sources of inputs (Gershon, 2000; Holtz-Bacha, 1997; Kranenburg, Cloodt, & Hagedoorn, 2001). Therefore, it also seems important to look at the international nature of diversification.

The sample of the companies that we study consists of large-sized publishing companies from Australia, Europe, and North America. We investigate the unidimensionality among the various diversification measures, while also taking the time dimension into account. Hence, in this study, we make a distinction between diversity, which measures the extension to which firms are simultaneously active in many distinct businesses at a point of time, and diversification, which measures changes in diversity over time. Because of the increasing importance of international expansion, we construct an additional measure to show the international diversification of these companies. This measure is related to Varadarajan and Ramanujam's (1987) two-dimensional measure based on broad and mean narrow spectrum diversity.

This article is organized as follows. The next section describes the literature on various diversification measures. The data set will be described in the following section, after which we present the results of this study. The last section covers the discussion of the results and some major conclusions to be drawn from of this study.

THEORETICAL BACKGROUND OF DIVERSIFICATION MEASURES

Development and maintenance of competitive advantages involve managerial decisions regarding what activities, businesses, and technologies the company should target for investment, relative to the investments made by competing companies (Geringer, Beamish, & daCosta, 1989). The type of diversification strategy that is used by the firm partly depends on the relatedness of these new products, markets, and technologies with its present ones. Product diversification, defined as expansion into product markets new to the company, has been a highly popular strategy among large and growing companies. However, given the degree of international activities of most companies, both in sales and in production, many are confronted with the choice for international or domestic diversification. This choice implies not only that companies have to decide whether they intend to operate in other businesses domestically or internationally, but that once a choice for international diversification is made, companies still have to consider a certain concentration on particular countries or international regions (Hitt, Hoskisson, & Ireland, 1994).

The literature explains the reasons for a diversification strategy according to a number of motives. Diversification may facilitate the deployment of resources and thereby enhance efficiency. The effective and efficient resource deployment encompasses two fundamental elements of any company's strategy: the range and relatedness of the products sold and the company's relative emphasis on foreign versus domestic operations (Geringer, Beamish, & daCosta, 1989). Amihud and Lev (1981) and Markides (1995) motivate corporate diversification in terms of the reduction of dependence on a few products and markets while limiting the effects of uncertainty in markets and technological developments. Thus, the essence of diversification is taken to be an expansion into new businesses and markets, requiring the development of new competences or the augmentation of existing ones. Another motive that is more intangible refers to the aspiration and goals of top management. Managers can also motivate diversification with the reduction of the probability of bankruptcy in order to provide job security and preserve their firm-specific human-capital investment (Amit & Livnat, 1988).

The sheer volume of research on diversification is an indication of the importance and relevance of the topic. Reflecting this phenomenon is the corresponding rise in the number of measures and techniques of firm diversification (Sambharya, 2000). The most accepted and most popular measures of diversification are based on discrete and continuous business count approaches (e.g., Jacquemin & Berry, 1979; Kim, 1989; Varadarajan & Ramanujam, 1987) and on the categorical (strategic) approach as popularized by Wrigley (1970) and Rumelt (1974). However, the literature is inconclusive in showing which diversification measure has to be used. Previous studies show that findings may depend upon the kind of measure that is used. Hoskisson and Hitt (1990) give a detailed overview of the measurement problems involved in using diversification measures. Clearly each of the methods of measuring corporate diversification has unique advantages and problems. Given the measurement differences, it is important to first study the existence of possible discrimination between the various measures before some inference with regard to corporate diversification can be made (Chatterjee & Blocher, 1992; Sambharya, 2000).

Diversification Measures

The categorical (strategic) approach. The categorical (strategic) approach is a subjective way of measurement. Central to this method is the conceptualization of the core activities of the company. Building on the work of Wrigley (1970), Rumelt (1974) categorized four major diversification strategy categories of large companies. These major categories are single business, dominant business, related business, and unrelated business. These categories provide a spectrum of diversification strategies of companies that diversify significantly into related businesses compared to companies that remain essentially undiversified. The categorization can be based first on the specialization ratio (Rs), which expresses the proportion of a firm's revenues attributable to its largest single business in a given year, and second on the related ratio (Rr), which expresses the proportion of a firm's revenues attributable to its largest group of related business. Specialized business diversification means that a company is basically committed to a single business ($Rs \geq 0.95$ & $Rr \geq 0.70$). Dominant business diversification refers to companies that diversified to only a limited extent from the single business ($0.70 \leq Rs < 0.95$ & $Rr \geq 0.70$). Related diversification of nonvertically diversified firms involves expansion into businesses related to the company's core activities ($Rs < 0.70$ & $Rr \geq 0.70$). Unrelated diversification of nonvertically diversified firms includes entry into businesses and markets unrelated to a company's previous activity ($Rs < 0.70$ & $Rr < 0.70$). Rumelt subdivided these four main categories further into subcategories characterizing the different diversification strategies of companies. This further differentiation is based on the pattern of linkages among the business lines of firms (see Rumelt, 1974, p. 11–32).

This approach has two major disadvantages. First, it demands detailed business-level information from numerous fragmentary sources such as annual reports, newspapers, specialized business reports, and other publications; in other words, this method is very time-consuming. Second, the categorical approach is based on understanding the underlying logic behind the firm's intentions and the assumed relatedness between businesses. Hence, this measurement depends very heavily on the qualitative assessment of diversification patterns.

The business count approach.   The argument in support of business count measures has drawn on the objectivity of the measurement method. These measures of diversification are built on established classification systems in which each of a firm's establishments is classified according to its primary classification or activity. Examples of established systems are the Standard Industrial Classification (SIC) system, which classifies all types of economic activities, and the regional classification system, which divides the world into regions. In addition, these objective measures deal with the degree of diversity, whereas the categorical (strategic) diversification measure focuses on the type of diversity. These business count models can therefore investigate within group differences. Continuous measures are variants of the formula diversification $= \sum m_i W_i$, where m_i is the percent of a firm's ith classified group revenues or sales, and W_i is an assigned weight summed over all a firm's classified groups (Chatterjee & Blocher, 1992). One of the most popular objective methods is the modified Berry–Herfindahl index (Montgomery, 1982). It relies on a classification system to assess the extent of the firm's operations in different classified groups. The modified Berry–Herfindahl index can be defined as follows:

$$\textit{Berry–Herfindahl diversification} = 1 - \left(\sum_j m_{ij}^2 \right) / \left(\sum_j m_{ij} \right)^2 \quad j = 1, \ldots, M,$$

where m_{ij} = proportion of jth classified group to ith firm's total sales, and M is the number of classified groups in which a firm operates. In this measure, if a firm operates in a single classified group, the Berry–Herfindahl index of diversification is zero and it becomes close to 1 if the firm's total sales are divided equally among any number of classified groups.

Another continuous count method for measuring diversification is the entropy approach. The entropy measure of diversification weights each m_{ij} by the logarithm of $1/m_{ij}$ and can be defined as follows:

$$\textit{Entropy index of total diversification} = \sum_j m_{ij} \, ln\left(1 / m_{ij} \right) j = 1, \ldots, M.$$

This measure is designed to decompose the total diversification measure into managerially meaningful elements of total diversification: unrelated and related diversification, international (related and unrelated) market diversification (Jacquemin & Berry, 1979; Kim, 1989). The modified Berry–Herfindahl diversification index cannot be decomposed as directly as entropy measure in additive elements that define the contribution of diversification at each level of classified group aggregation to the total. Like the modified Berry–Herfindahl index of diversification, the entropy index of total diversification also yields a score of zero for single classified group firms and becomes greater with increasing levels of diversification.

Another popular business count method is the discrete two-dimensional categorical diversification measure developed by Varadarajan and Ramanujam (1987). It is a simpler and more objective method of Rumelt's category measure. A feature of this conceptualization is that it does not require data on sales or revenues of activities, but still provides insights into both the degree of diversification and its direction. This method distinguishes between two distinct patterns of diversification to capture Rumelt's classification: mean narrow spectrum diversification (MNSD) and broad-spectrum diversification (BSD). Varadarajan and Ramanujam define BSD as the number of 2-digit SIC codes in which a firm concurrently participates. MNSD is defined as the number of four-digit SIC codes a firm operates in divided by the number of two-digit SIC categories in which the firm participates. This method treats BSD and MNSD as the two dimensions of a four-cell matrix, where each cell represents the totality of a firm's past diversification activities in various two- and four-digit industry categories. The matrix contains the following cells: firms with very low diversity are classified in cell A, B contains related diversified firms, C represents unrelated diversified firms, and firms with very high diversity are grouped in cell D.

In analyzing global diversification, however, this measure is not satisfactory because it is not able to deal with international market dimensions. It is therefore important to construct a measure for international diversification. Using the two-dimensional conceptualization of diversity developed by Varadarajan and Ramanujam (1987), we suggest a diversification measure across international geographic areas. Our conceptualization treats geographic market areas as the primary classified groups, defining also the mean narrow spectrum international diversification (MNSID) and the broad-spectrum international diversification (BSID). The employed international-count measure of diversification is built on the modified Eurostat (2003) classification (see the appendix). The BSID is defined as the number of superregions in which a firm concurrently operates, whereas the MNSID measure is defined as the number of subregions in which a firm operates divided by the number of superregions in which it participates. The MNSID represents the diversification of a company into geographic areas closely related to each other, that is, regions within a broader area. On the other hand, BSID—across superregions—represents diversification into areas either unrelated to or less closely related to each other. We can also present a two-dimensional matrix in which each cell represents the totality of a firm's past diversification activities in various super- and subgeographic areas. Figure 1 shows the two-dimensional conceptualization of international diversity.

Broad Spectrum International Diversity*	High	Cell C: International unrelated-diversified firms	Cell D: Firms with very high international diversity
	Low	Cell A: Firms with very low international diversity	Cell B: International related-diversified firms
		Low	High
		Mean Narrow Spectrum International Diversity**	

FIGURE 1   Classification system of international diversification strategies. *Note.* *Broad spectrum international diversity is defined as the number of superregions in which a firm concurrently participates in. **Mean narrow spectrum international diversity is defined as the number of subregions a firm operates in divided by the number of superregions the firm participates in.

A desirable feature of our proposed conceptualization is that it does not require data on international sales or revenues of geographic markets. However, it still provides insights into the degree of internationalization, that is, high versus low, and the direction of internationalization, that is, predominantly concentrated in one geographic area or predominantly internationally diversified.

DESCRIPTION OF SAMPLE AND DATA

For the empirical analysis of product and international diversification in the publishing industry we have chosen large-sized publishing companies from Australia, Europe, and North America. According to Worldscope, the selected companies are among the highest revenue generating companies in the industry. Another argument for choosing large-sized companies is the current level of competition between these companies and the importance of their international activities. The years under investigation are 1999 and 2002. We have selected 32 companies that are active in the publishing industry. Missing data on divisional revenues and primary business codes or a categorization of revenues that did not correspond with our classification system reduced the number of observations available for most of our analyses to 30 companies. The sample consists of 1 Australian, 15 European, and 14 North American companies. The data set is mainly compiled from information published by the companies and some additional sources. Data on (international) geographic presence and revenues as well as revenues per activity are based on annual reports. The following eight categories of industrial activities are used in this study: books, magazines, newspapers, entertainment, marketing, education, the Internet, and other activities. The international revenues are classified under domestic, Europe, North America, and the rest of the world. Due to the limitation of the available data, we could not classify the revenues in smaller categories. We obtained information on the numbers of two- and four-digit SIC categories in which companies operated from Worldscope and Osiris.

We use the revenues per activity and geographic area to calculate the continuous diversification measures. The computation of the discrete count measure for the product diversification is based on two- and four-digit SIC codes, and the international diversification measure is based on the modified Eurostat/European Union classification (see the appendix). We classify firms into the four cells using the mean values of BS(I)D and MNS(I)D as cut-off points to establish low–high splits along each dimension as proposed by Varadarajan and Ramanujam (1987). The revenues per activity and the SIC codes are also used to classify the diversification strategy of the companies according to Rumelt's categories. Given the available data we are only able to classify companies in the four main diversification strategy categories. The basic statistical techniques used for comparing the various diversification measures in our study are Pearson correlations and chi-square statistics.

RESULTS

Table 1 reports the calculated diversification measures of the publishing companies based on their activities. The first group of columns reports the diversity of the publishing companies in the year 1999, and the second group reports the diversity in 2002. The Rumelt measure demonstrates that the majority of the firms are diversified in related businesses. A few companies are basically committed to a single business or diversified to only a limited extent from the single business. Lagardère is the only company following an unrelated diversification strategy. It is also active, for example, in the automobile industry, aerospace industry, and defense industry. The indicated Rumelt classification for 2002 is generally similar to the classification of 1999. Only a few companies have changed their diversification strategy into a more related one or a dominant business one. It seems that the Varadarajan and Ramanujam (V&R) classification differs slightly from the indicated Rumelt's classification. Based on the SIC-codes, V&R results for 1999 classified 19 publishing companies into the C category, which indicates unrelated diversified firms, while the findings of 2002 classified the firms more equally between the four cells.

The continuous diversification measures, the Berry–Herfindahl index, and the entropy index show similar diversity of the publishing companies and also a movement in the same direction over time. The values of the Berry–Herfindahl and the entropy measures are between 0 and 0.76 and between 0 and 1.50 respectively. The publishing companies Knight Ridder and Trinity Mirror operated

TABLE 1
Measurement Results of Activity Diversification of Publishing Companies for 1999 and 2002

Company	Year 1999						Year 2002					
	Rumelt	SIC BSD	SIC MNSD	SIC V&R	BH	Entropy	Rumelt	SIC BSD	SIC MNSD	SIC V&R	BH	Entropy
Axel Springer (Germany)	RBD	1	5.00	B	.57	0.96	RBD	1	1.00	A	.65	1.26
Banta (U.S.)	RBD	4	1.25	C	.66	1.08	RBD	5	1.40	C	.73	1.34
Belo (U.S.)	RBD	3	1.00	C	.50	0.74	RBD	4	1.50	D	.52	0.81
Bertelsmann (Germany)	RBD	5	1.60	C	.76	1.50	RBD	2	2.00	B	.66	1.22
Canwest (Canada)	SBD	1	2.00	B	.00	0.00	RBD	1	1.00	A	.49	0.69
Daily Mail and General Trust (England)	DBD	3	1.33	C	.23	0.46	RBD	2	1.00	A	.48	0.79
Emap PLC (England)	DBD	3	1.33	C	.45	0.77	RBD	1	2.00	B	.49	0.90
E. W. Scripps (U.S.)	RBD	3	1.33	C	.53	0.87	RBD	2	2.00	B	.55	0.87
Gannett (U.S.)	DBD	3	2.33	D	.24	0.40	DBD	3	2.33	D	.21	0.37
Hollinger (Canada)	RBD	1	2.00	B	.50	0.70	RBD	1	2.00	B	.50	0.69
Independent News & Media (Ireland)	SBD	3	1.67	C	.00	0.00	RBD	1	1.00	A	.64	1.14
Knight Ridder (U.S.)	SBD	3	1.67	C	.00	0.00	SBD	2	1.00	A	.04	0.10
Lagardère (France)	UBD	5	1.40	C	.13	0.25	UBD	2	1.50	B	.61	1.12
Lee Enterprises (U.S.)	DBD	3	1.00	C	.36	0.54	DBD	2	1.00	A	.34	0.57
McGraw-Hill (U.S.)	RBD	4	1.25	C	.49	0.68	RBD	3	2.00	D	.50	0.69
Meredith (U.S.)	RBD	3	1.67	C	.65	1.08	DBD	3	2.00	D	.38	0.57
The News Corporation (Australia)	RBD	3	1.67	C	.58	1.15	RBD	3	1.67	D	.52	1.05
Pearson (England)	RBD	4	1.25	C	.65	1.21	RBD	2	1.00	A	.54	1.02
Primedia (U.S.)	RBD	1	3.00	B	.55	0.94	RBD	2	1.50	B	na	na
Reader's Digest (U.S.)	RBD	2	1.50	A	.48	0.67	RBD	5	1.80	D	.65	1.07

(continued)

TABLE 1 (Continued)

Company	Year 1999						Year 2002					
	Rumelt	SIC BSD	SIC MNSD	SIC V&R	BH	Entropy	Rumelt	SIC BSD	SIC MNSD	SIC V&R	BH	Entropy
Reed Elsevier (England/The Netherlands)	RBD	2	2.00	B	.50	0.69	DBD	2	2.50	B	.32	0.50
Sanoma WSOY (Finland)	RBD	3	1.33	C	.73	1.43	RBD	3	1.33	C	.71	1.37
Schibsted (Norway)	RBD	3	1.33	C	.48	0.68	DBD	1	1.00	A	.38	0.77
The Thomson Corporation (Canada)	RBD	3	2.00	D	.50	0.86	RBD	1	1.00	A	.60	1.00
Trinity Mirror (England)	SBD	1	1.00	A	.06	0.13	DBD	1	1.00	A	.07	0.17
United News and Media (England)	RBD	3	1.67	C	.62	1.04	RBD	1	1.00	A	na	na
VNU (The Netherlands)	RBD	3	1.67	C	.58	1.03	RBD	1	1.00	A	.61	1.00
Washington Post Company (U.S.)	RBD	4	1.50	C	.58	0.98	RBD	4	1.50	D	.73	1.34
Wegener Arcade (The Netherlands)	RBD	3	2.00	D	.73	1.35	DBD	1	2.00	B	.40	0.69
Wolters Kluwer (The Netherlands)	RBD	3	1.67	C	.71	1.30	RBD	1	1.00	A	0.74	1.37

Note. The nationality of the company is in parentheses. SIC BSD = standard industrial classification broad-spectrum diversification; SIC MNSD = standard industrial classification mean narrow spectrum diversification; SIC V&R = standard industrial classification Varadarajan and Ramanujam classification; BH = Berry-Herfindahl; B = related-diversified firm; A = firm with very low diversity; C = unrelated-diversified firm; D = firm with very high diversity; RBD = related business diversification; SBD = single business diversification; DBD = dominant business diversification; UBD = unrelated business diversification.

mainly in one business, newspapers, in the periods 1999 and 2002, whereas the companies Independent News & Media and Canwest became more diversified. Bertelsmann was the most diversified publishing company in 1999 and Wolters Kluwer in 2002. However, the values of these indexes may be dominated by the category of other activities. For instance, these findings now suggest that the company Lagardère is a low diversified firm, although it operates in many unrelated businesses. In general, the majority of selected companies have their main activities in the information and communications markets, and therefore the continuous measures seem to be a good indication of the diversified activities of the publishing companies.

With regard to the international-based diversification, the Berry–Herfindahl and entropy indexes again show similar results. Table 2 reports the calculated diversification measures of the publishing companies based on their international activities. The first group of columns reports the international diversity of the publishing companies in the year 1999, and the second group reports the international diversity in 2002. The values of the Berry–Herfindahl and entropy indexes are between 0 and 0.71 and between 0 and 1.28 respectively. The findings show that, in particular, the U.S. publishing companies—Belo, E. W. Scripps, Knight Ridder, Lee Enterprise, Meredith, and Primedia—mainly focus their activities on their home market. The publishing companies from other countries are more internationally focused. The highest internationally diversified companies are Bertelsmann, Largardère, Hollinger, and VNU with minimum Berry–Herfindahl and entropy values of 0.61 and 1.03 respectively. The international diversity values are relatively stable over time, which indicates that the publishing companies did not change their international diversification strategy in the last couple of years. This is also confirmed by the international geographic spectrum diversification results (see column international V&R). Based on the geographic areas, the evidence shows that the number of companies with a very low international diversity and internationally diversified firms has been the same for the investigation period. However, a few international geographic diversified publishing firms have changed their international diversification strategy. For instance, VNU changed from an internationally related diversified firm into a very high internationally diversified firm.

The purpose of this study is not only to show the diversity of publishing companies but also to compare the various diversification measures. In order to discover whether these different diversification indicators are related to each other, statistical methods are used to analyze the existence of a relationship between the indicators. The first test to investigate the comparison between the various measures is the Pearson correlation coefficients.

Table 3 reports the Pearson correlation coefficients among the business count measures that were utilized in the study. The results show that the relationship between entropy and the Berry–Herfindahl indexes are positive and significant. The

TABLE 2
Measurement Results of International Diversification of Publishing Companies

Company	Year 1999					Year 2002				
	BSID	MNSID	INT V&R	BH	Entropy	BSID	MNSID	INT V&R	BH	Entropy
Axel Springer (Germany)	2	2.00	B	.23	0.39	1	3.00	B	.28	0.45
Banta (U.S.)	3	1.00	A	.23	0.47	3	1.00	A	.27	0.53
Belo (U.S.)	1	1.00	A	.00	0.00	1	1.00	A	.00	0.00
Bertelsmann (Germany)	7	2.29	D	.71	1.28	7	1.86	D	.70	1.25
Canwest (Canada)	4	1.00	C	.52	0.80	5	1.00	C	.13	0.29
Daily Mail and General Trust (England)	5	1.40	C	.27	0.56	6	1.50	C	.34	0.66
Emap PLC (England)	6	1.17	C	.62	1.08	6	1.50	C	.47	0.80
E. W. Scripps (U.S.)	1	1.00	A	.00	0.00	2	1.00	A	.00	0.00
Gannett (U.S.)	5	1.00	C	.09	0.18	5	1.20	C	.22	0.38
Hollinger (Canada)	1	1.00	A	.62	1.03	1	1.00	A	.62	1.03
Independent News & Media (Ireland)	4	1.00	C	.55	0.93	3	1.33	A	.59	0.99
Knight Ridder (U.S.)	1	1.00	A	.00	0.00	1	1.00	A	.00	0.00
Lagardere (France)	7	1.57	D	.70	1.28	4	3.50	D	.70	1.28

Company										
Lee Enterprises (U.S.)	1	1.00	A	.00	0.00	1	1.00	A	.00	0.00
McGraw-Hill (U.S.)	7	1.71	D	.32	0.61	3	1.67	B	.32	0.61
Meredith (U.S.)	1	1.00	A	.00	0.00	1	1.00	A	.00	0.00
The News Corporation (Australia)	6	2.17	D	.41	0.74	4	2.00	D	.38	0.69
Pearson (England)	4	1.00	C	.58	1.07	5	2.20	D	.45	0.89
Primedia (U.S.)	2	1.00	A	.00	0.00	2	1.00	A	na	na
Reader's Digest (U.S.)	6	1.67	D	.50	0.69	6	1.50	C	.50	0.69
Reed Elsevier (England/The Netherlands)	6	1.17	C	.62	1.13	4	1.25	C	.54	1.03
Sanoma WSOY (Finland)	5	1.60	D	.15	0.34	5	1.60	D	.54	0.88
Schibsted (Norway)	1	3.00	B	.49	0.69	1	3.00	B	.51	0.75
The Thomson Corporation (Canada)	5	1.20	C	.31	0.65	5	1.60	D	.33	0.67
Trinity Mirror (England)	1	1.00	A	.01	0.04	1	1.00	A	.01	0.04
United News and Media (England)	3	1.00	A	.56	0.91	3	1.00	A	.52	0.87
VNU (The Netherlands)	3	1.67	B	.68	1.22	7	2.71	D	.61	1.11
Washington Post Company (U.S.)	6	1.00	C	.48	0.67	2	1.00	A	.08	0.17
Wegener Arcade (The Netherlands)	1	3.00	B	.24	0.41	1	2.00	B	.19	0.33
Wolters Kluwer (The Netherlands)	4	1.50	D	.52	0.81	4	1.50	C	.55	0.86

Note. The nationality of the company is in parentheses. BSID = broad-spectrum international diversification; MNSID = mean narrow spectrum international diversification; INT V&R = international Varadarajan and Ramanujam; BH = Berry–Herfindahl; B = related-diversified firm; A = firm with very low diversity; D = firm with very high diversity; C = unrelated-diversified firm.

99

TABLE 3
Pearson Correlations of Business Count Diversification Measures for 1999 and 2002

Variables	M	SD	BHI	BSD	MNSD	IEM	IBHI	BSID	MNSID
Year 1999									
EM	0.783	0.421	0.974**	0.286	0.087	0.134	0.111	0.089	0.378*
BHI	0.460	0.230		0.229	0.095	0.109	0.100	0.036	0.347
BSD	2.867	1.074			−0.487**	0.299	0.246	0.444*	0.178
MNSD	1.714	0.751				−0.060	−0.054	−0.097	0.146
IEM	0.599	0.430					0.985**	0.601**	0.221
IBHI	0.347	0.252						0.556**	0.242
BSID	3.667	2.218							0.073
MNSID	1.402	0.579							
Year 2002									
EM	0.874	0.349	0.964**	0.206	−0.165	0.476*	0.488**	0.355	0.347
BHI	0.502	0.184		0.222	−0.095	0.458*	0.466*	0.368	0.257
BSD	2.100	1.213			0.324	−0.245	−0.235	0.042	−0.259
MNSD	1.468	0.485				0.049	0.044	0.061	−0.176
IEM	0.594	0.405					0.987**	0.605**	0.514**
IBHI	0.339	0.236						0.565**	0.510**
BSID	3.333	2.023							0.209
MNSID	1.564	0.700							

Note. BHI = Berry–Herfindahl index; BSD = broad-spectrum diversity; MNSD = mean narrow spectrum diversity; IEM = international entropy measure; IBHI = international Berry–Herfindahl index; BSID = broad-spectrum international diversity; MNSID = mean narrow spectrum international diversity; EM = entropy measure.
*Correlation is significant at the .05 level (two tailed). **Correlation is significant at the .01 level (two tailed).

high correlation is to be expected because these indexes are based on almost the same information. However, the evidence does not show a significant relationship between the international and the activity-based Berry–Herfindahl and entropy indexes. It is interesting to see that there is a positive statistical significant correlation between the international Berry–Herfindahl and entropy indexes and the BSID measure. Thus, the correlation findings indicate that it does matter which business count method is used to measure the degree of diversification of publishing companies. It seems that the different diversification indicators measure dissimilar aspects of diversification.

The chi-square test is used to compare the Rumelt's diversification classification and the V&R classification of the publishing companies. Table 4 demonstrates the chi-square results for 1999 and 2002 concerning the Rumelt results and the activity- and international-based V&R results. It shows a strong relationship between the activity-based measures, also over time. However, no relationship exists between the international measure and the two activity-based measures in both years. This test demonstrates that the activity-based and international-based nonmetric measures are two completely different measures in determining diversification levels of publishing companies.

TABLE 4
Chi-Square Test for Comparison Between Rumult's and Varadarajan and
Ramanujam's Diversification Classifications

Diversification Indicators	Year 1999			Year 2002		
	χ^2	df	Asymptotic Significant	χ^2	df	Asymptotic Significant
Rumelt	33.2	3	0.000	35.6	3	0.000
Varadarajan and Ramanujam activity measure	28.4	3	0.000	8.1	3	0.043
Varadarajan and Ramanujam international measure	2.8	3	0.423	4.4	3	0.221

Note. Expected cell frequency is 7.5.

DISCUSSION AND CONCLUSIONS

We have applied various diversification measures to indicate the activities, international geographic diversity, and diversification strategy of publishing companies. Statistical analyses are applied to compare the various diversification measures with each other. Not only do these different analyses indicate similar developments, they also complement each other in terms of specific information that is generated. In that sense this study provides a rather comprehensive picture of recent diversification developments in the international publishing industry and its large-sized players.

What we have learned is that the large-sized publishing companies from Australia, Europe, and North America do indeed diversify into a number of activities and businesses related to information and communication services and products. We also notice that the diversity of publishing companies varies between both years. A few companies changed their diversification strategy in the period under investigation, although the majority of publishing companies followed an unchanged diversification strategy. No distinction can be made between the product diversification strategies of companies coming from different geographic areas. However, a clear distinction can be made when looking at the international diversification strategy of these companies. A relatively large number of North American companies mainly focused their operations on their home market. They did not follow such an international diversification strategy, whereas companies from the other areas did follow an international diversification strategy. Due to the large home market, it is possible that these North American companies do not have to focus on international markets to maintain their competitive advantages or to survive. Furthermore, because the momentum of new technological developments and new businesses largely lies in the United States, companies from outside North America have no alternative but to also focus outside their home markets. In particular the leading European companies have gone through a transition from traditional companies, mainly operating in their domestic markets, to companies that also operate in important international markets.

Our findings regarding the different diversification measures, indicating the level of diversified activity and the degree of internationally based diversification in this sample, are inconclusive. A disparity was found between the set of diversification measures. It is clear that the activity-based diversification indicators measure other aspects of diversification than the international-based measures. Even within these two groups, their indicators measure different aspects of diversification. The Berry–Herfindahl and entropy indexes represent somewhat different aspects of diversification than the two spectrum diversification measures. Furthermore, the two nonmetric activity-based diversification indicators, Rumelt's classification and the V&R's classification, measure likely similar aspects of diversification. The international-based nonmetric measure does not. The international-based group is comprised of measures that can be used interchangeably to measure diversification, although the relationship with MNSID is weak.

This study reveals the strengths and weaknesses of various product and international diversification measures. Although one measure may be more appropriate than the other for particular research, when considering all issues involved in variable selection and measurement, no indicator is clearly superior to the others. It is obvious that a single measure may not be able to capture all the nuances and subtleties of any given diversification strategy. Our findings confirm the results from other studies that have suggested the use of multiple measures of diversification in the measurement of strategy variables (Hoskisson & Hitt, 1990; Sambharya, 2000).

Our findings do imply that there is need for additional, context-informed analyses. Further research could consider a number of topics relevant for understanding the measurement of diversification. An obvious item for further research is to investigate the impact of the current indicators in the publishing industry. Clearly each of the methods of measuring product and international diversification measures a particular aspect of diversification. Given the measurement differences, it is important to decide which measures to take before some inference with regard to corporate diversification can be made (Chatterjee & Blocher, 1992).

As part of the continuous effort to build better theories and improved models to understand the motives for diversification, it is appealing to focus on the effect that the diversification strategies of publishing companies, both activity- and international-geographic oriented strategies, have on their performance. Publishing companies are confronted with the decision of how to deploy their resources for competitive advantage. They can diversify based on relatedness of businesses or activities to increase their performance or they can achieve the same result through international geographic diversification.

Finally, it is important to note that our findings relate to very large publishing companies from Australia, Europe, and North America. Further research should test the relevance of our findings for a sample of small and medium-sized publishing companies or for publishing companies from other geographic areas.

ACKNOWLEDGMENTS

Hans van Kranenburg thanks the Media Management and Transformation Centre at the Jönköping International Business School for its hospitality and the Netherlands Foundation for Scientific Research (NWO) for providing financial support.
We gratefully acknowledge the research assistance of Hanneke ter Velde and Kim Wolters in collecting the data for this article.

REFERENCES

Amihud, Y., & Lev, B. (1981). Risk reduction as a managerial motive for conglomerate mergers. *Bell Journal of Economics, 12*, 605–617.

Amit, R., & Livnat, J. (1988). A concept of conglomerate diversification. *Journal of Management, 14*(4), 593–604.

Bennett, J. (1999). Discovering America again. *Magazine for Magazine Management, 18*, 53–59.

Chatterjee, S., & Blocher, J. D. (1992). Measurement of firm diversification: Is it robust? *Academy of Management Journal, 35*(4), 874–888.

Eurostat (2003). *Geonomenclature.* Methods and Nomenclatures, European Commission.

Geringer, J. M, Beamish, P. W., & daCosta, R. C. (1989). Diversification strategy and internationalization: Implications for MNE performance. *Strategic Management Journal, 10*, 109–119.

Gershon, R. A. (2000). The transnational media corporation: Environmental scanning and strategy formation. *Journal of Media Economics, 13*(2), 81–101.

Hitt, M. A., Hoskisson, R. E., & Ireland, R. D. (1994). A mid-range theory of the interactive effects of international and product diversification on innovation and performance. *Journal of Management, 20*(2), 297–326.

Holtz-Bacha, C. (1997). Development of the German media market: Opportunities and challenges for US media firms. *Journal of Media Economics, 10*(4), 39–58.

Hoskisson, R. E., & Hitt, M. A. (1990). Antecedents and performance outcomes of diversification: A review and critique of theoretical perspectives. *Journal of Management, 16*, 461–509.

Jacquemin, A. P., & Berry, C. H. (1979). Entropy measure of diversification and corporate growth. *Journal of Industrial Economics, 27*(4), 359–369.

Kim, W. C. (1989). Developing a global diversification measure. *Management Science, 35*(3), 376–383.

Lanic. (2003). *Countries in Latin America & the Caribbean*, Retrieved June 17, 2003, from the World Wide Web: http://www.lanic.utexas.edu/subject/countries.html

Markides, C. C. (1995). *Diversification, refocusing and economic performance.* Cambridge, MA: MIT Press.

Montgomery, C. A. (1982). The measurement of firm diversification: Some new empirical evidence. *Academy of Management Journal, 25*(2), 299–307.

Rumelt, R. P. (1974). *Strategy, structure, and economic performance.* Boston: Harvard Business School Press.

Sambharya, R. B. (2000). Assessing the construct validity of strategic and SIC-based measures of corporate diversification. *British Journal of Management, 11,* 163–173.

van Kranenburg, H. L., Cloodt, M., & Hagedoorn, J. (2001). An exploratory study of recent trends in the diversification of Dutch publishing companies in the multimedia and information industries. *International Studies of Management and Organization, 31*(1), 64–86.

Varadarajan, P. R., & Ramanujam, V. (1987). Diversification and performance: A reexamination using a new two-dimensional conceptualization of diversity in firms. *Academy of Management Journal, 30*(2), 380–393.

Wrigley, L. (1970). *Divisional autonomy and diversification.* Unpublished doctoral dissertation, Harvard Business School.

APPENDIX

The geographic classification of the world was developed by the European Union for classifying all regions of activities for the EU members. As far as possible, this classification system should conform to the actual structure of the world based on the treaties and trade associations.

TABLE A
Geographic Classification of the World Into Super- and Subregions

Superregions	Subregions
Europe	European Union, Central and Eastern European Countries, and European Free Trade Association
Middle East	Mediterranean Countries in the Euro-Mediterranean Partnership, The Gulf,[a] and Commonwealth of Independent States
North and Central America	North American Free Trade Association, and Central America
South America	The Andean Community, Mercosur, and Caribbean[b]
Africa	West Africa, Central Africa, East Africa, The Horn of Africa, Indian Ocean Islands, and Southern Africa[c]
Asia	Northeast Asia, South Asian Association for Regional Cooperation, and Association of Southeast Asia Nations
Australia and Pacific	Australia and Pacific[d]

[a]Iraq, Iran, and Yemen are grouped into the Gulf region, because of proximity. [b]Cayman Islands, Puerto Rico, and Virgin Islands are classified as Caribbean (Lanic, 2003). [c]Chile is classified in the Mercosur as it is geographically closest to it. [d]Because of its geographic proximity, Guam is grouped together with the Pacific region. Source: Eurostat/European Union (2003).

The Effect of New Networks on U.S. Television Diversity

Daniel G. McDonald and Shu-Fang Lin
School of Communications
The Ohio State University

Communication researchers in general, and media researchers in particular, have devoted considerable effort to the analysis of diversity. In the area of mass communication, issues of programming, ownership, economics, and competition have all been linked to the concept of diversity or its counterpart, diversification. McDonald and Dimmick (2003) have noted that the constructs of diversity, variety, and diversification can all be measured using the same indices and indicate the same underlying concept. In addition, concentration is typically measured using the reverse of common measures of diversity and therefore also refers to the same underlying concept. For this reason, we will use the more general term of diversity in this article.

Many studies of diversity are descriptive in nature, conducted with the goal of examining diversity under particular conditions. In the case of simple descriptive studies, the reporting of a particular level of diversity using any of a number of indices is sufficient. A few studies have gone beyond these descriptive efforts to track diversity under varying conditions.

Virtually all of these studies, however, have been limited by a lack of appropriate statistical tests. As a result, the claims that can be made are typically couched in phrases such as "diversity *appears to be* different in the two conditions (or time periods, etc.)." Some studies use an "eyeball" approach in comparing data and report "significant differences," even when no statistical tests have been made. However, a visual comparison of diversity levels is very similar to visually comparing means; statistically significant differences cannot be determined by the level of diversity any more than an examination of means can be used to assess statistically significant differences in mean values.

Requests for reprints should be sent to Daniel G. McDonald, School of Communication, The Ohio State University, 154 N. Oval Mall, Columbus, OH 43210. E-mail: mcdonald.221@osu.edu

If the field of communication research is to advance beyond descriptive studies of diversity, it will be important to assess true statistically significant differences so that theoretically driven hypotheses can be tested, and variation in diversity may be attributed to specific characteristics or conditions. This article reviews the method and use of statistically significant differences in diversity. We first examine the idea of dual-concept diversity, then examine Simpson's D (Simpson, 1949) and its extensions, explain the conditions in which D or its variants might be applied, and then use U.S. network television data to illustrate the utility of powerful diversity measures.

DUAL-CONCEPT DIVERSITY

We follow Junge's (1994) notion that diversity is a two-dimensional concept (see also McDonald and Dimmick, 2003). The first dimension is typically a set of discrete classification categories; the second is the number or proportion of objects allocated to these classifications. Thus, for example, in a study of diversity in media ownership, race of the owners of media outlets might be the categorical dimension, whereas the second dimension would be the percentages or proportions of owners of each race, with the totals adding to 1.00 or 100%.

A measurement goal for researchers studying diversity is to incorporate a diversity measure that expresses these two dimensions in a single number. In essence, that number should reflect the interaction of the number of categories with the distribution of elements within those categories. Typically, that interaction has been conceptualized such that a perfectly flat distribution of objects allocated to categories should be the most diverse, and a distribution in which all of the objects are allocated to one category is the least diverse.

Although single-concept measures have been used in the literature (e.g., DeJong & Bates, 1991; Dominick & Pearce, 1976; Long, 1979), we will not consider these measures. McDonald and Dimmick (2003) point out some of the problems with interpretability of any single-concept measure of diversity. Because there is no shortage of dual-concept measures (McDonald & Dimmick [2003] describe 13 dual-concept measures), this article limits consideration to dual-concept measures.

For this study, we follow the logic expressed in McDonald and Dimmick (2003), that a measure of diversity should have the two following highly desirable characteristics: (a) the measure (or its standardized version) should vary between 0 and 1.00, with 0 indicating no diversity and 1.00 indicating the most diverse distribution possible, and (b) adding additional categories to which no population members are assigned should not change the value of diversity. To this list we add a third desirable characteristic: (c) variance within the measures should be partitionable so that analyses may focus on contributions of other variables to diversity or tests for statistically significant differences. Of the 13 measures reviewed by McDonald and Dimmick (2003), only Simpson's D and Shannon's H have had sufficient study to be known to have these three characteristics (Agresti & Agresti, 1977; Good, 1953; Teachman, 1980).

SIMPSON'S D

Simpson's D $\left(\hat{D} = 1 - \sum_{i=1}^{k} \hat{p}_i^2 \right)$ has one additional characteristic that Shannon's H does not have—ease of interpretability. Simpson's D is obtained by summing the squared probabilities (the p_i's) from all the categories and subtracting that sum from 1.0. The diversity value obtained is equivalent to the probability that two of the objects of classification (the elements), chosen at random, would be in different categories. If all the objects are in one category, then the probability is 0, as is the diversity measure; if all of the objects are in different categories, then Simpson's D is 1.0, which corresponds to the probability that all the objects are in different categories. For this reason, we prefer the use of Simpson's D, and will use D and an extension, Lieberson's D_b (Lieberson, 1969), for illustrative purposes in this article. Calculation and hypothesis testing formulae are available in the appendix.

Simpson's D is a very strong candidate for a general measure of diversity. The fact that it varies between 0 and 1, and that its value at a given point is also a readily understandable probability, seem to be inherent strengths of the measure that no other diversity measure offers. It is therefore useful and straightforward in simple descriptive studies in which the researcher is interested in a single measure of diversity. In addition, the measure is readily interpretable across studies because it always indicates the same thing: the probability that two elements, selected at random from the population, are in different categories.

An additional strength is provided by a standardized version. One of the continual difficulties in social science research is that the categories of classification may be different for different studies, even those studies examining the same phenomenon. One difficulty in interpretation of a probabilistic measure is that, in practice, we almost never have the same number of categories as elements to be classified, so the probability will not be 1.0—the maximum is determined by the number of categories: max = (k - 1)/k, where k = the number of categories. Thus, a population with 10 categories has a greater potential for diversity (max = .9) than a population with 3 categories (max = .67). However, a standardized version of D can be calculated quite easily by dividing by its theoretical maximum: $D_Z = D/(1 - 1/k)$, and that transformation yields a value that corrects for different numbers of categories in different studies, making comparisons across studies a simple task.

In addition to making simple comparisons of the D value obtained in different studies or for different groups, and so on, the variance of D is known and can be calculated easily with a hand calculator (see appendix). Because of this, confidence intervals can be constructed around the obtained values of D, just as they can with means, percentages or probabilities. In addition, simple hypothesis tests involving differences between groups are easy to conduct, as are tests of null hypotheses of specific values (e.g., a value from a previous study).

There have also been a number of extensions of D to aid specific comparisons or hypotheses. The first extension of D we will consider was developed by Lieberson (1969), and is generally referred to as Lieberson's D_b. Lieberson's D_b is used in the case of two different populations and represents the probability that two elements selected randomly, one from each population, are classified differently on the categorical variable (Agresti & Agresti, 1977). Such a measure is highly useful in comparing two populations to see how similar or dissimilar they are in the categories of classification (see appendix).

The second and third extensions of D are used in situations in which populations are classified according to two or more nominal variables (Agresti & Agresti, 1977). The second extension is known as Multivariate D (D_{multi}), and is used in cases in which a single population may be classified using two different variables. D_{multi} represents the average proportion of the two variables on which the two elements differ in classification (Agresti & Agresti, 1977; Lieberson, 1969).

The third extension is referred to as Multivariate D_b, D_{bmulti}, also developed by Lieberson (1969). D_{bmulti}, is similar to D_{multi} and also represents the proportion of different classifications of a sampled pair on two variables, but, in this case, the pairs are chosen from two different populations. D_{multi} and D_{bmulti} are thus similar to D and D_b, respectively, except that they allow multiple variables of classification. Although the calculation is correspondingly more complex, it may still be done with a hand calculator or spreadsheet (appendix).[1]

APPLICATION OF POWERFUL DIVERSITY MEASURES

For this article, we examine diversity in U.S. television programming from 1986 to 2000, a period that saw the growth of a number of new networks through cable and broadcast, or a combination of the two. For our purposes, we consider a new network to be successful if it offers at least one program that attracts an audience rating high enough to be included in the Nielsen yearend summary of average ratings for the year. We illustrate the range of diversity over the study years and assess the extent to which the successful new networks affected overall diversity of television programming offerings and the diversity of programming on the three traditional networks.

---

[1]Interested readers who prefer to use Shannon's H as a measure are referred to Teachman (1980), who provides the statistical properties and interpretation for Shannon's H.

In the competitive arena of television programming, one can imagine several different scenarios when new networks become successful. On one hand, if they become successful with an innovation of a particular type of program, the traditional networks may imitate that program. Typically, the rise of a new program type signals the demise of a different type, and so diversity could remain fairly constant even while the dominant program types exhibit change (Dominick & Pearce, 1976; McDonald & Dimmick, 2003; McDonald & Schechter, 1988).

On the other hand, the traditional networks may not imitate a competitor's innovative format, and, if that is the case, system diversity should increase slightly. If each new competitor specializes in an innovative new format, and the traditional networks do not imitate those new formats, overall system diversity should increase substantially. Another scenario might suggest that traditional networks may innovate under competition, and so traditional networks may grow more diverse regardless of whether the new networks are innovative or not.

However, it could also be the case that the new networks may be generalists and offer program types that are already present; in such a situation, if the new networks offer those program types in approximately the same distribution as traditional networks, overall diversity would not change. An altogether different process could occur in which, as new, specialist networks become successful, traditional networks become specialists as well. In such a case, the individual network diversity will be low, but overall system diversity could be high.

These scenarios all point to a basic issue in assessing system-level diversity. High system-level diversity can be achieved if all the networks are generalists, all specialists, or some generalists and some specialists. Policy related to program offerings should take into account that there are multiple ways to achieve diversity. We use the U.S. television network system to illustrate this point and to move diversity analyses beyond descriptive studies.

The research literature has addressed this issue in limited ways. Owen, Beebe, and Manning (1974, p. 130), for example, appear to assume that the addition of a fourth network to the three traditional networks should increase program diversity. Long's (1979) historical study of the early 1950s (when the DuMont network competed with ABC, NBC, and CBS) suggests that the decline of a fourth network lead to lower program diversity. However, Long's conclusion, derived from studying the first years of a developing medium, may not be applicable to the situation of competition within a mature medium.

The question typically is described in terms of competition. Litman (1979) analyzed U.S. television in the 1970s, a period of increased network competition, and found that increased competition led to increased diversity. A number of studies however, have found the opposite relation when examining competition and diversity (Lin, 1995a, 1995b; Liu, 1997).

The key may be in a more careful specification of the concepts involved in the relationships. Competition may be from new competitors, or it may be within the oligopoly itself. Litman's (1979) finding of increased diversity related to competition studied competition within the oligopoly (i.e., between the traditional networks). Lin (1995a) compared a period of competition within the oligopoly (the 1970s) to a period of competition with new alternatives from outside the oligopoly (cable and VCRs in the 1980s), and found a decline in diversity among the networks. An additional study by Lin (1995b) also found that increased external competition reduced diversity. Li and Chiang (2001) again found that diversity of network programming declined in the advent of competition from satellite and cable television.

Findings from studies of media other than television offer similar results. Burnett (1992) found that competition within the radio industry was negatively related to diversity; Berry and Waldfogel (2001) found that increased concentration of radio station ownership increased diversity of radio formats within a market, as did Rogers and Woodbury (1996). Similarly, a study of the videocassette industry by Hellman and Soramaki (1985) found a negative relationship between competition and diversity.

We suggest that these results, taken together, suggest that competition within an oligopoly leads to increased diversity of programs within that oligopoly, whereas competition from outside competitors leads the members of the oligopoly to rely on "tried and true" measures to maintain market share, thus decreasing diversity within the members of the oligopoly. We thus should have a television system in which overall system diversity will increase under competition (due to the innovation of new networks) while diversity within the traditional networks will decrease.

We therefore offer the following hypotheses for the U.S. television industry during the period of 1986 to 2000:

H1: Overall system diversity will increase in the period between 1986 and 2000.
H2: Traditional network diversity will decrease between 1986 and 2000.

As described earlier, there are multiple ways in which system-level diversity can be affected. We also offer the following research questions to address patterns of diversity that may be developing within the television industry.

RQ1: Do the new networks offer more, less, or about the same level of diversity in programming as traditional broadcast networks?
RQ2: Are the successful new networks specialists or generalists in their offerings?
RQ3: Has the advent of new networks altered the degree of specialization of the three traditional networks?

METHOD

We included every network program listed in the A. C. Nielsen yearend summary of first-run programs offered on network television (published in May or early June in a number of sources).[2] From 1986 through 1988, only programs in the three traditional broadcast networks were listed in the Nielsen rating summary: ABC, NBC, and CBS. In the late 1980s, the Fox network was created from a number of independent television stations. With diffusion of cable, these stations began to reach a wide audience. By 1989, shows on the Fox network were listed in the yearend summary. In the 1990s, the UPN, WB, and PAX cable network programs appeared in the list (see Figure 1).

We classify Fox, UPN, WB, and PAX as new nontraditional networks for this study. The impact of the new networks is apparent in the number of programs appearing in the Nielsen lists, which increased dramatically from 1986 to 2000. In 1986, the Nielsen summary included 81 programs; in 2000, the summary included 196 programs (Table 1).

Program type was added to the lists of programs in an iterative fashion. First, all of those programs included in Brooks and Marsh (1999) were given the program type listed. If a program was not listed in Brooks and Marsh, two internet resources provided a program type for the bulk of the remaining programs: TV Tome (http://www.tvtome.com/) and All Your TV (http://www.allyourtv.com/showguides.html). After consulting these three sources, a few programs were still not classifiable, but a direct search of the Internet by the program name yielded a program type for all of the remaining programs.

Because many of the program type classifications are idiosyncratic or highly specific (the earlier mentioned method yielded 151 program types), the authors developed a general program type scheme using 24 program types and combined the 151 types into the 24 general types.[3] These 24 types were used in the present analysis.

ANALYSIS

Simpson's D was computed for each year of the study period (1986–2000) in several different ways: overall system diversity (based on the distribution of all pro-

---

[2]Sources used to obtain the yearly listings were yearend averages published in *Electronic Media* and *Variety*. Program types were obtained from Brooks and Marsh (1999), TV Guide online, tvtome.com, and allyourtv.com.

[3]The program types used in this study were Adventure, Animal, Anthology, Game, Cartoon, Comedy, Detective, Documentary, Drama, Foreign Intrigue, Fantasy, Informational, Movie, Music, Newsmagazine, Police, Public Service, Reality, Religion, Science Fiction, Sports, Supernatural, Variety, and Western.

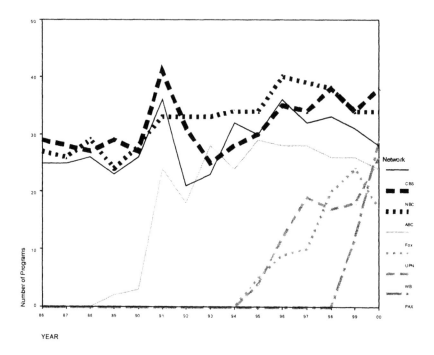

FIGURE 1   Number of programs by network.

TABLE 1
Television System Diversity in 1986 and 2000

Variables	1986	2000
Traditional networks		
CBS	25	28
NBC	29	38
ABC	27	34
Number of programs	81	100
Traditional net diversity	.790	.770
Variance of diversity	.002	.031
New networks		
Fox	0	24
UPN	0	17
WB	0	26
PAX	0	29
Number of programs	0	96
New net diversity	—	.840
Variance of diversity	—	.017
Total		
Number of programs	81	196
Total system diversity	.790	.820
Variance of diversity	.002	.004

grams in the yearly summary of programs), individual network diversity (diversity for each network, each year it was on), traditional network diversity (diversity of all programs offered by ABC, NBC, and CBS each year), and new network diversity (diversity of all programs offered by Fox, UPN, WB, and PAX). Because all comparisons involve the same number of program type categories, there is no need to standardize D. In addition, because there are 24 program types, the maximum possible D value is .96; a standardized value of D will be very close to the unstandardized values presented here.

Lieberson's D_b is used to measure between-network diversity. Lieberson's D_b also offers ready interpretability, because it represents the probability that two elements drawn randomly, one from each population, are classified differently. In the special case in which the two populations have identical distributions, D_b is equivalent to D. The appendix includes the details regarding confidence intervals and hypothesis testing with D.

RESULTS

Our first hypothesis suggested that overall system diversity should increase between 1986 and 2000. Figure 2 presents a graphical illustration of the trend in di-

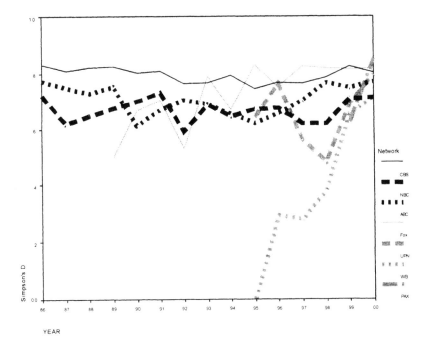

FIGURE 2   Diversity levels for all seven networks.

versity between 1986 and 2000 for each of the seven networks, and Figure 3 provides an illustration of the aggregate diversity for the traditional networks, the new networks, and overall system diversity. A visual examination of these figures suggests change in the system. It appears that the new networks very quickly become as diverse as traditional networks. In fact, from 1993 to 2000, the Fox network, one of the new networks, was the most diverse of all.

Overall system diversity (the solid line in Figure 3) appears to decline from 1986 to about 1993, and increase from 1997 onward, a time period coinciding with the growth of the new networks. All three lines (overall, traditional and new networks) increase during that time period. As is evident from an examination of Figure 3, there appears to be a slight increase in diversity for traditional networks, but the diversity level in 2000 is not as high as overall system diversity or diversity among the new networks. This suggests that the new networks are more diverse than traditional networks, and the success of the new networks has been the major factor responsible for the increase in overall system diversity during the study period. Traditional network diversity appears to decline slightly during the study period.

To examine these changes in depth we turn to statistical tests. Table 1 presents diversity data between 1986 and 2000. In 1986, the traditional networks (the only

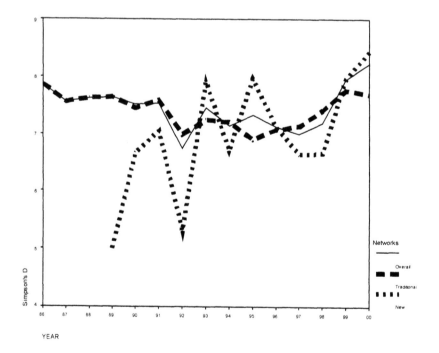

FIGURE 3   Diversity levels for the overall system, traditional and new television networks.

networks appearing in the yearend summary) had a diversity level of .79 with 81 programs. In 2000, the traditional and new networks combined had a diversity level of .82 with 196 programs in the summary. A test for a significant difference (simply a test that the confidence interval in the difference in diversity between 1986 and 2000 did not include zero—see the appendix) between system diversity in 1986 and 2000 was significant—the 95% confidence interval is (.02, .04), indicating that overall system diversity was higher in 2000 than in 1986.

Our second hypothesis suggested that there should be a change in diversity of programs offered by the traditional networks. Again, Table 1 provides the relevant data—the hypothesis test for a difference is simply a test between the 1986 value (.79) and the 2000 value for the traditional networks (.77). In this case, the 95% confidence interval for the difference ranges between -.03 and .04, which means that zero is included within the confidence interval, so we cannot reject the hypothesis of no difference.

Thus far, our tests have shown a significant increase in overall system diversity, but no change in diversity for the traditional networks. Our first research question asked whether the new networks offer a different level of diversity in programming than do the traditional networks. In this case, the comparison is a diversity level of .77 (traditional networks in 2000) compared to a diversity level of .84 (new networks in 2000). The 95% confidence interval for the difference between the two types of networks is (.03, .11), which does not include zero. We therefore conclude that there is a significant difference between the new networks and traditional networks, with the new networks more diverse than traditional networks.

As previously mentioned, greater diversity can be obtained with networks being either generalists or specialists, so we tested for specialization of the new networks (Research Question 2). We first calculated individual network diversity for all seven networks and system diversity separately for the traditional and new networks. If greater diversity has been achieved by new network specialization, then Simpson's measure should be relatively low for each of the new networks, while their combined diversity should be high. If they are generalists, then we should expect no significant difference between an individual network's diversity level and the overall diversity of the group in which it belongs.

Table 2 provides the diversity level for each of the seven networks in 2000, as well as overall system diversity for the traditional and new networks and between-group diversity for traditional and new networks. Our first test showed that only the WB network diversity level was significantly different from the overall new network diversity level of .84. In this case, the WB network diversity level, at .72, was significantly lower, suggesting that WB offers more specialized programs, whereas the other new networks are more general in their offerings.

Other data related to specialization is presented in the network/own group and network/other group comparison sets of D_b statistics presented in Table 2. Although we do not present all the statistical comparison tests here (because of the

TABLE 2
Network Diversity

Variables	Traditional Networks			New Networks			
	ABC	CBS	NBC	Fox	PAX	UPN	WB
Within-group diversity							
Network diversity 1986	.77	.83	.72	—	—	—	—
Network diversity 2000	.77	.80	.71	.82	.85	.80	.72[a]
Overall within-group diversity 1986		.79			—		
Overall within-group diversity 2000		.77			.84[b]		
Between-group diversity							
Network/own group 1986 Lieberson's D_b	.57	.62	.57	—	—	—	—
Network/own group 2000 Lieberson's D_b	.77[c]	.80[c]	.75[c]	.85	.80	.84	.89
Network/other group 2000 Lieberson's D_b	.85	.84	.84	.83	.82	.78	.92
Traditional/new networks 2000 Lieberson's D_b				.84			
1986 multivariate Simpson's D_{multi}		.73			—		
2000 multivariate Simpson's D_{multi}		.72			.81		

[a]Indicates a significant difference between diversity for the WB network in comparison to overall diversity of the new networks. [b]Indicates a significant difference between traditional and new network diversity in 2000. [c]Indicates a significant difference in between-group diversity in comparing 1986 to 2000.

number of comparisons), we present the data for expository purposes and provide two of the possible tests. In the network/own group 2000 comparisons, the D_b figures range from .77 to .80 for the traditional networks, and .80 to .89 for the new networks, suggesting that there is more specialization among the new networks than among the traditional networks (higher D_b values indicate a greater degree of specialization). In the network/other group comparison, values range from .84 to .85 for traditional networks, and .78 to .92 for the new networks, suggesting that a network like WB (with a value of .92) is highly differentiated from the traditional networks, whereas UPN, with a between-group diversity value of .78 comparing it to traditional networks, and .84 comparing it to the new networks, is more like the traditional networks in its offerings than it is like the new networks in their offerings ($p < .05$).

Our final research question asked whether the advent of successful new networks had altered the degree of specialization of the traditional networks. To test this proposition, for both 1986 and 2000, we calculated Lieberson's D_b (between-group diversity) for each of the traditional networks in comparison to the overall traditional network diversity. D_b provides an index of the extent to which the networks "mirror" each other in their distributions. If they are specialists, D_b will be high, as there will be little similarity in the proportion of programming allotted to various program types. If the networks have altered their degree of specialization as a result of the new networks, we should find a significant difference between the 1986 and 2000 between-group diversity levels. As indicated in Table

2, all three networks have significant differences in comparing 1986 and 2000, supporting the idea that the traditional networks have had to specialize in the wake of competition from new networks. This is especially interesting in light of the test involving analysis of overall diversity levels, which have not changed.

We confirmed the conclusion of specialization without a change in system diversity with a second test designed to assess change in overall diversity of the three traditional networks. Table 2 also provides the D_{multi} values for the three traditional networks in 1986 (.73) and 2000 (.72). The D_{multi} treats network as a variable, rather than as a population, and tests for overall diversity within levels of that variable. A test of differences shows no statistically significant difference between the two years, again suggesting that the traditional networks have not altered their level of diversity as a result of the success of new nontraditional networks, even though they are more specialized.

DISCUSSION

As diversity continues to be of central concern in communication research, it is important for communication scientists to pay careful attention to the concept and its measurement. There were a number of substantive findings from our illustrations that have implications for policy as well as for understanding network programming. Using national U.S. television network program data from 1986 to 2000, we have explored five research questions and have been able to get a reasonable grasp of the relation between network competition and program diversity during this time period.

What we have found is that the new networks have resulted in more than double the number of programs classified in the Nielsen annual summaries of television, and there has been a concomitant increase in overall system diversity. Although overall diversity has increased, the traditional television networks have remained fairly constant in their level of diversity. The new cable and other nontraditional channels rose quickly to levels comparable to those of the traditional broadcast networks and, within a few years, surpassed the traditional networks' program diversity.

In light of the rise of the new networks, the traditional networks have apparently begun to specialize somewhat; all three traditional networks show greater between-group diversity in 2000 than was evident in 1986.

We discussed several possible ways in which system diversity can increase. One of these ways is to have a number of networks that specialize in particular content types. Our tests showed that this has not been the case for traditional networks taken as a group, but appears to be so for all of the new networks. That is, even though the traditional networks have each specialized, their content repertoire has not grown more diverse, suggesting that, as a group, traditional network content is about as diverse as it was before the advent of the new networks, but individually they appear to be specializing in certain content types.

In terms of the new networks, the WB network is significantly less diverse than the other new networks as a group, and the between-group diversity involving WB and traditional networks was not significantly different from overall diversity for traditional networks. However, all of the new networks, including the WB, are significantly more specialized than are the traditional networks.

The other new networks all appear to have a broad range of content, suggesting that the newer networks, which are more diverse than traditional networks, must attain that diversity through emphasizing program types that are underemphasized in traditional networks—bringing greater diversity to the system while maintaining specialization.

Although researchers have talked about the possibility of a television of abundance for decades now, and of the implications of cable for program diversity, this study has attempted to document how the past decade and a half have played out in terms of that diversity. Although it is clear that there are many cable and other networks that are highly specialized (HGN, the Food Network, etc.), they are not yet represented in annual Nielsen summaries. The new networks that are represented—that is, those that have developed programs that attract large enough audiences to be included in the summaries—are clearly generalists. Predictions that technology has ended or will end "mass" communication are not yet borne out—mass communication channels still dominate television entertainment.

This article has sought to suggest how the use of one of the better measures of diversity, Simpson's D, has a number of advantages over descriptive measures, including its potential in statistical analyses. We hope that the results obtained from our analyses, and the implications of the results for understanding network program diversity in the era of competition, offers a strong rationale for the use of more advanced techniques, not only in the study of network television, but in many areas in which diversity plays a key part.

REFERENCES

Agresti, A., & Agresti, B. F. (1977). Statistical analysis of qualitative variation. In K. F. Schuessler (Ed.), *Sociological methodology 1978* (pp. 204–237). San Francisco: Josey-Bass.

Berry, S. T., & Waldfogel, J. (2001). Do mergers increase product variety? Evidence from radio broadcasting. *Quarterly Journal of Economics, 116*(3), 1009–1025.

Brooks, T., & Marsh. E. (1999). *The complete directory to prime time network and cable TV shows.* New York: Ballantine.

Burnett, R. (1992). The implications of ownership changes on concentration and diversity in the phonogram industry. *Communication Research, 19,* 749–769.

DeJong, A. S., & Bates, B. J. (1991). Channel diversity in cable television. *Journal of Broadcasting & Electronic Media, 35*(2), 159–166.

Dominick, J. R., & Pearce, M. C. (1976). Trends in network prime-time programming, 1953–1974. *Journal of Communication, 20,* 70–80.

Good, I. J. (1953). The population frequencies of species and the estimation of population parameters. *Biometrika, 40,* 237–264.

Hellman, H., & Soramaki, M. (1985). Economic concentration in the videocassette industry: A cultural comparison. *Journal of Communication, 35*(3), 122–134.

Junge, K. (1994). Diversity of ideas about diversity measurement. *Scandinavian Journal of Psychology, 36,* 16–26.

Li, S. C. S., & Chiang, C. C. (2001). Market competition and programming diversity: A study on the TV market in Taiwan. *Journal of Media Economics, 14*(2), 105–119.

Lieberson, S. (1969). Measuring population diversity. *American Sociological Review, 34,* 850–862.

Lin, C. S. (1995a). Diversity of network prime-time program formats during the 1980s. *Journal of Media Economics, 8*(4), 17–28.

Lin, C. S. (1995b). Network prime-time programming strategies in the 1980s. *Journal of Broadcasting & Electronic Media, 39,* 482–495.

Litman, B. R. (1979). The television networks, competition and program diversity. *Journal of Broadcasting, 23*(4), 393–410.

Liu, Y. L. (1997). *Multiple TV channels and their audiences.* Taipei, Taiwan: Shyr-Ying.

Long, S. L. (1979). A fourth television network and diversity: Some historical evidence. *Journalism Quarterly, 56,* 341–345.

McDonald, D. G., & Dimmick, J. (2003). The conceptualization and measurement of diversity. *Communication Research, 30*(1), 60–79.

McDonald, D.G., & Schechter, R. (1988). The audience role in the evolution of fictional television content. *Journal of Broadcasting & Electronic Media, 32*(1), 61–71.

Owen, B. M., Beebe, J. H., & Manning, Jr., W. G. (1974). *Television economics.* Lexington, MA: Lexington.

Rogers, R. P., & Woodbury, J. R. (1996). Market structure, program diversity, and radio audience size. *Contemporary Economic Policy, 14*(1), 81–91.

Simpson, E. H. (1949). Measurement of diversity. *Nature, 163,* 688.

Teachman, J. D. (1980). Analysis of population diversity. *Sociological Methods & Research, 8,* 341–362.

APPENDIX
Formulas for Diversity and Statistical Inferences

1. To calculate Simpson's D and compare D for two groups:
a. Calculation of Simpson's D

$$\hat{D} = 1 - \sum_{i=1}^{k} \hat{p}_i^2$$

where k refer to a number of categories in the distribution; p_i is the proportion in the ith category ($i = 1, \ldots, k$).

b. Calculation of confidence interval for two groups

$$\left(\hat{D}_2 - \hat{D}_1\right) \pm Z_{a/2} \sqrt{\left(\hat{\sigma}_1^2 / n_1\right) + \left(\hat{\sigma}_2^2 / n_2\right)}$$

where

$$\hat{\sigma}_1^2 = 4 \left[\sum_{i=1}^{k_1} \hat{p}_i^3 - \left(\sum_{i=1}^{k_1} \hat{p}_i^2 \right)^2 \right]$$

$$\hat{\sigma}_2^2 = 4 \left[\sum_{i=1}^{k_2} \hat{q}_i^3 - \left(\sum_{i=1}^{k_2} \hat{q}_i^2 \right)^2 \right]$$

n_1 is the number of observations in the sample of the first population. k is the number of categories in the distribution. p is the proportion in the ith category ($i = 1$, ..., k_1), and D_1 is the index of diversity.

n_2 is the sample size selected from another population and divided into k_2 categories. The proportions corresponding to the categories are $\{q_i, 1 \le i \le k_2\}$, and the index of diversity is D_2.

2. To calculate Lieberson's D_b and compare two groups:
a. Calculation of confidence interval

$$D_b \pm Z_{a/2} \sqrt{\frac{\sum_{i=1}^{k} \hat{p}_i \hat{q}_i^2}{n_1} + \frac{\sum_{i=1}^{k} \hat{q}_i \hat{p}_i^2}{n_2} - \frac{\left(n_1 + n_2\right)\left(1 - \hat{D}_b\right)}{n_1 n_2}}$$

where

$$D_b = 1 - \sum_{i=1}^{k} \hat{p}_i \hat{q}_i$$

$$\hat{\sigma}_b^2 = \left(\frac{n_1 + n_2}{n_1}\right) \sum_{i=1}^{k} \hat{p}_i \hat{q}_i^2 + \left(\frac{n_1 + n_2}{n_2}\right) \sum_{i=1}^{k} \hat{q}_i \hat{p}_i^2 - \frac{\left(n_1 + n_2\right)^2}{n_1 n_2} \left(\sum_{i=1}^{k} \hat{p}_i \hat{q}_i \right)^2$$

n_1 is the number of observations in the sample of the first population. k_1 is the number of categories in the distribution. p_i is the proportion in the ith category ($i = 1$, ..., k_1). n_2 is the sample size selected from another population and divided into k_2 categories. The proportions corresponding to the categories are $\{q_i, 1 \le i \le k_2\}$.

b. Calculation of test statistic

$$Z = \sqrt{n_1 + n_2} \left(\hat{D}_b - D_b^{(0)}\right) / \hat{\sigma}_b$$

3. To calculate the Multivariate D:
a. Calculation of confidence interval

$$\left(\hat{D}_2 - \hat{D}_1\right) \pm Z_{a/2} \sqrt{\left(\hat{\sigma}_1^2 \middle/ n_1\right) + \left(\hat{\sigma}_2^2 \middle/ n_2\right)}$$

where

$$\hat{D} = 1 - \left(\sum_{i=1}^{k_1} \hat{p}_i^2 + \sum_{i=1}^{k_2} \hat{p}_i^2 + \ldots + \sum_{i=1}^{k_m} \hat{p}_i^2\right) \middle/ m$$

$$\hat{\sigma}^2 = \left(4 \middle/ m^2\right) \left[\sum_i \hat{p}_i \left(\hat{p}_{i_1} + \ldots + \hat{p}_{i_m}\right)^2\right] - 4\left(1 - \hat{D}\right)^2$$

m is the number of variables. The lth of the variables has k_l levels, $l = 1, 2, \ldots, m$. p_i is the proportion of the population in cell i.

Cultural Diversity in the Movie Industry: A Cross-National Study

François Moreau
Laboratoire d'Econométrie
Conservatoire National des Arts et Métiers, France

Stéphanie Peltier
MATISSE University of Paris 1 and
University of La Rochelle, France

For many years, the promotion and preservation of cultural diversity has remained a core issue in international debates about free trade. In this article we propose a framework to assess cultural diversity that is used to compare this diversity in the movie industry between 1990 and 2000 in the European Union, United States, France, Hungary, Mexico, and South Korea. Our main results are (a) the ranking of the countries is highly dependent on the dimensions of cultural diversity considered; (b) cultural diversity turns out to be higher in countries where the movie industry receives strong public support (France, European Union, South Korea); and (c) supplied diversity and consumed diversity are positively correlated, and the former is always higher than the latter. This evidence suggests that a policy that supports cultural diversity on the supply side seems to match consumers' preferences.

Globalization is claimed to pose a grave threat to cultural diversity. This is the position adopted during debates within the World Trade Organization (WTO) by those who argue that the exchange of cultural goods and services should be treated as an "exception" to the application of free trade. Considered as restrictive and protectionist, the term "exception", which first appeared during the Uruguay Round, was subsequently replaced by the term "diversity." A group of countries, led by France, thus proposed that cultural diversity should be established as a principle of international law, calling for the adoption by the international community, under the aegis

Requests for reprints should be sent to François Moreau, Laboratoire d'Econométrie, Conservatoire National des Arts et Métiers, 2 Rue Conté, 75003, Paris, France. E-mail: moreauf@cnam.fr

of UNESCO, of an international agreement on cultural diversity. The underlying rationale of such an agreement is that public welfare is better served by more potential and effective choices as reflected in higher diversity. But what is cultural diversity? How can we measure it? Although it has become a widely adopted credo, the concept of "cultural diversity" is particularly polysemous. States, international organizations, and multinational media groups all use this term without really meaning the same thing. Does diversity refer to the number of works released, the number of works consumed, the geographical origin of cultural products … ? The possible meanings are numerous. Yet, within a context of ever-increasing concentration of the international market of cultural industries, the ability to measure cultural diversity is indispensable to evaluate both the consequences of this concentration and the effectiveness of cultural policies. Hence, the need for an instrument of evaluation of the multiple facets of cultural diversity, enabling international comparisons to be made, has become crucial. However, to our knowledge, no study has yet attempted to carry out an international comparison of cultural diversity in any given industry. Our aim in this article is thus to propose and test a practical tool for the diagnosis of the condition and evolution of cultural diversity on a national and on an industry level. Of course, we don't intend to raise here the issue of the scope of "culture." Should this scope be restricted to cultural industries such as movie, television, publishing, or music? Or should it be broadened, as does UNESCO, to all the activities that are more or less connected with the cultural traditions of a country (food, health, clothing, sport …)? Though this debate is much beyond the scope of this article, do notice that the methodology we proposed remains workable whatever the scope of "culture" is. In the first analysis, however, the application of our proposed tool is limited to the film industry, the field in which the debate on free trade is the most heated. Moreover, the study has been carried out for only six countries or geographical zones (France, Hungary, Mexico, South Korea, the United States of America, and the European Union) over the period 1990–2000.

Economists have already thoroughly explored the question of diversity in two different fields: that of biodiversity (Metrick & Weitzman, 1998; Solow, Polasky, & Broadus, 1993; Weitzman, 1992, 1993, 2000) and that of technological diversity (Cohendet, Llerena, & Sorge, 1992; Frenken, Saviotti, & Trommetter, 1999; Saviotti, 1996). In both cases, the central issue is one of arbitration between the costs and advantages of maintaining diversity compared with a situation of standardization. In the field of bioculture, for example, there is a long-standing trade-off between concentrating on high-yield varieties and maintaining sufficient diversity to lower the risks of catastrophic infection (Weitzman, 2000). Clearly, the construction of a tool for measuring diversity is an indispensable preliminary step for tackling this question. The most successful of these tools was developed by Weitzman (1992): We will look at it in more detail later. It has been used, for example by Frenken, Saviotti, and Trommetter (1999), to evaluate the evolution in technological diversity in four industries: planes, helicopters, motorcycles, and micro-computers. In the field of media, the question of diversity is essentially one of guaranteeing the plurality of opinions expressed by different organs of the press. The economic debate is thus focused on the danger that the concentration of the media will reduce the diversity of opinions expressed[1] (see, e.g., Iosifidis [1999]). If we restrict ourselves to cultural industries, the economic analysis of diversity has, as far as we know, given rise to relatively few contributions. Anderson (1992) analyzed the impact of Canadian television broadcasting quotas on the diversity of programming by type of program. Using an approach similar to our own, Van der Wurff (2002), Van der Wurff and Van Cuilenburg (2001), and Sarrina Li and Chiang (2001) have explored the link between intensity of competition and diversity of television programming. However, their definition of cultural diversity is quite restrictive. Moreover, they do not propose any measuring tool that could be used to draw international comparisons.

The following section is devoted to the methodology of the study, and more precisely to the choice of indicators of cultural diversity. We then present the data and results obtained. The discussion includes a commentary on the results and introduces the debate about the determining factors of cultural diversity (industry concentration, the promotional strategies of large groups, and public policy).

METHOD

The Three Dimensions of Diversity: Variety, Balance, Disparity

The literature devoted to biodiversity, technological diversity, or to the optimal diversity of a financial portfolio highlights three key properties of diversity (see Stirling [1999] for a survey). These three properties, which establish necessary but individually insufficient conditions to the existence of diversity, are variety, balance, and disparity. Variety refers to the number of categories into which a quantity can be partitioned (for instance the number of species from a biodiversity perspective). Balance refers to the pattern in the distribution of that quantity across the relevant categories. Disparity refers to the nature and the degree to which the categories themselves are different from each other. The greater the variety, the balance and the disparity of a system are, the larger its diversity. In the case of the film industry, these three dimensions of diversity can be presented in terms of three spe-

---

[1]See the debate on the role played during the spring of 2003 by the different media controlled by News Corp (notably various newspapers in the United States and Great Britain and the television company FoxNews) in the construction of public opinion in Anglo-Saxon countries on the subject of war in Iraq.

cies (or units of analysis): the film, the genre, and the geographical origin. Accord-ing to the first unit of analysis, each film is considered unique. Diversity then increases in direct proportion to the number of films, the level to which occupation of screens and shares in receipts are uniformly distributed between the films, and the extent to which the films are as "different" as possible. According to the second unit of analysis, the genre, diversity increases in direct proportion to the number of genres available (comedies, drama, cartoons, etc.), the extent to which they are equally well represented, and the extent to which the genres are clearly differenti-ated from each other. Finally, according to the third unit of analysis, geographical origin, film diversity in a given country increases in direct proportion to the num-ber of different geographical origins available, the extent to which these origins are equally well represented, and the extent to which they display marked specificities that distinguish them clearly from each other.

The quantitative assessment of variety and balance is straightforward: Variety is a simple positive integer, and balance is something close to variance. Disparity turns out to be much more difficult to assess. Whatever the subject of analysis is—biodiversity, technological diversity, or cultural diversity—the measurement of disparity first requires the establishment of a taxonomy, that is to say a parti-tion of a set of elements in exhaustive and separate categories. It is true that widely accepted taxonomies of cultural goods that could serve as the basis for analysis already exist (e.g., by genre or by geographical origin). However, a cru-cial problem arises: How can we analyze the mutual disparity between the dif-ferent categories in the taxonomy? A tool is required for evaluating the *distance* between the different films in terms of their genres or geographical origins. But the most successful economic studies, carried out by Weitzman (1992, 1993) in the field of the preservation of biodiversity, cannot be applied to the question of cultural diversity. The hypotheses put forward by Weitzman are unworkable here. The measurement of disparity he proposes is only effective for perfect tax-onomies, in other words, taxonomies whose distance is ultrametric (the disparity changes at an equal rate between the different branches of the taxonomy). We are faced with a double problem. In addition to the vast scale of the calculations required, highlighted by Solow, Polasky, and Broadus (1993), the hypothesis of ultrametric distance dramatically restricts the practical scope of such a tool. In the context of cultural diversity, this would mean, for example, that we would consider the disparity between a Korean film and a French film to be of the same scale as that between a Belgian film and a French film, or that the disparity be-tween a comedy and a drama is identical to that between a cartoon and a thriller! As such assertions are hardly acceptable, the question of the measurement of disparity remains unanswered. In terms of geographical origin, we could of course attempt to evaluate the distances between different countries on the basis of a multicriteria perspective: geographical position (bordering, same continent, different continent), level of development, official language, type of society

(Western, Eastern, etc.).[2] However, our position is that any attempt to quantitatively assess disparity between cultural products would be far too controversial and would only weaken the proposed tool.

These different considerations have led us to base our evaluation of cultural diversity solely on the criteria of variety and balance. It should, however, be noted that as far as we know no economic analysis of diversity has made use of all three criteria. In the field of technological diversity, priority is often given to variety (Cohendet, Llerena, & Sorge, 1992; Saviotti, 1996), whereas in the field of biodiversity only disparity is considered (Weitzman, 1992, 1993).

The Distinction Between Supplied Diversity and Consumed Diversity

In terms of cultural diversity, the supply and demand sides of the market each display their own specificities. It is therefore important to distinguish between the diversity supplied and the diversity consumed and to analyze the extent to which diversity supplied corresponds to the diversity consumed by the economic agents. This distinction raises a crucial question: Does an increase in the diversity supplied have a positive impact on the diversity consumed? In other words, to what extent do supplied and consumed diversities interact with each other?

This approach in terms of supplied and consumed diversity is similar to the distinction between open diversity and reflective diversity proposed by Van der Wurff and Van Cuilenburg (2001). Open diversity is calculated on the basis of the gap between production equilibrium and perfect theoretical equilibrium (equipartition of statistical individuals between the different categories). The smaller the gap, the greater the diversity. As for reflective diversity, it is calculated on the basis of the gap between production equilibrium and consumption equilibrium. Here again, a small gap means a high degree of diversity. Reflexive diversity thus measures the degree of response of supply to demand. While open diversity corresponds perfectly to the concept of supplied diversity, we believe reflective diversity to be a slightly more restrictive notion than consumed diversity. The postulate underlying reflective diversity is that the diversity supplied should reflect the diversity demanded. However, in the cultural industries it is not irrational to supply a greater level of diversity than will ultimately be consumed. As Caves (2000) underlines, faced with uncertainty about the future success of any given product (the "nobody knows" property of cultural products), it is rational to "overproduce" with the aim of maximizing the chances that one of the products will coincide with the desires

---

[2]For example, certain studies have attempted to measure the cultural distance between different countries by means of several criteria used to characterize a society of individuals: masculinity, individualism, aversion to uncertainty, or, again, the importance attached to the holding of power. For an application of such criteria, see, for example, Kogut and Singh (1988).

of the consumers. Furthermore, relying on the concept of reflective diversity would validate the strategy of the large film companies, aiming to reduce the number of films produced each year while locking the demand for each film through massive advertising campaigns. Such a strategy clearly runs counter to the objective of increasing cultural diversity. We have therefore preferred to use a distinction between supplied and consumed diversity.

What is the definition of cultural diversity that emerges from this discussion? We have just shown that cultural diversity should not be equated solely with the preservation or development of nationally produced works in the supply and demand of cultural products within a country—although it often is. For us, the cultural diversity proposed in a country should be taken to mean the quantitative and qualitative diversity of the production and consumption of cultural goods and services. In other words, cultural diversity represents the possibility that consumers have to enjoy access to a large supply of cultural products (in terms of quantity), comprised of diversified segments (in terms of genres and geographical origins) of relatively well-balanced sizes. It also represents the effective consumption of these numerous and diversified cultural products.

The Variables Used

Hence, ideally, the assessment of cultural diversity in the movie industry should rely on both supplied and consumed diversity and on three dimensions (variety, balance, and disparity) and on three units of analysis (individual film, genre, geographical origin), giving a $2 \times 3 \times 3$ matrix. We have explained why we believe it preferable to omit the dimension of disparity. Given the lack of statistical data on the genres of films supplied and consumed in most countries, we have also had to abandon the "genre" unit of analysis. The assessment of cultural diversity proposed in this article will thus focus on both supplied and consumed diversity, on two dimensions (variety and balance), and on two units of analysis (film and geographical origin). However, even this $2 \times 2 \times 2$ matrix of indicators of cultural diversity in the film industry cannot be perfectly completed.

In terms of variety, only the "film" unit of analysis has been used. The variety supplied is measured by the number of films released[3] in a given country in one year. This variable indicates the size of the supply of different films. However, it is essential to cross this "theoretical" supply with an indicator of the accessibility of the supply. Is it offered to the greatest possible number of consumers or reserved for an elite? Measurement of the variety supplied is thus completed by the number of screens available for every 100,000 inhabitants. The higher this number is, the

---

[3]We consider the number of films released during the year in the country in question and not the number of films produced, which, by definition, only reflects the supply of national and coproduced films, and not the overall supply of films, from all origins.

greater the chances, a priori, that each film will be widely available in space (geographical coverage) and time (number of days the films are shown). On the consumption side, an intense level of demand is a necessary condition for the existence of diversity. Intense demand maximizes the chances that each variety supplied will be consumed. The variety consumed is thus evaluated on the basis of average admissions per capita. In the matter of variety, both supplied and consumed, the "geographical origin" unit of analysis has been left out, because the data available obliged us to use taxonomy of "domestic films/American films/other films."[4] In other words, the dimension of variety has been neutralized because the result is three for every country in the sample.

Balance is studied using the two units of analysis "film" and "geographical origin." From the perspective of the geographical origin of films (both supplied and consumed), balance is measured using the Herfindhal-Hirschmann index (HHI), traditionally used to measure industrial concentration in a market. This reflects the degree of concentration of the films released and cinema admissions for the three listed geographical origins. It should be noted that the HHI is, in reality, an indicator that simultaneously measures variety and balance. $\text{HHI} = \sum s_i^2$ where s_i is the market share of each statistical individual. Thus, the HHI depends not only on the balance, of course, but also on the number of individuals. When two firms have equal shares in a market, the HHI is higher than when three firms all have equal shares in the same market. However, in our case, as the number of individuals is always three—the three geographical zones—the HHI is simply an indicator of balance. The higher the value of the index, the weaker the balance.[5] Balance is also analyzed at the film level. We thus look at the distribution of admissions over the total number of released movies. This is an indicator of consumed diversity that makes it possible to study whether consumers tend all to go and see the same films or, on the contrary, each film obtains a similar audience. We thus calculate the CR_{10},[6] in other words, the market share of the top 10 films in the total number of admissions. An equivalent indicator for supplied diversity should take into account the concentration of copies per film. Here we would look at the distribution of the total number of copies over the movies released. This would enable us to measure the degree of inequality in the competition between the different films. Unfortunately, this datum is not available at the present time for all the countries in the sample.[7]

---

[4]This represents the lowest common denominator of the different countries in the sample. Of course, much more precise classification is possible for some countries, notably France.

[5]The three-dimensional typology used results in a minimal value of the HHI of 3,267 (maximum balance) and a maximum value of 10,000 (minimum balance).

[6]It is impossible to calculate the HHI in this case because the complete set of data on the distribution of admissions by film is unavailable for most countries.

[7]The French National Film Centre supplies these data for France, but they are unavailable for other countries.

Table 1 summarizes the different variables used and gives a good idea of the progress that remains to be made to achieve an exhaustive measurement of cultural diversity in the film industry.

DATA

The study analyses six countries or geographical zones over the period 1990–2000. The United States, France, and the European Union have been chosen because they are at the heart of the heated debates over cultural diversity that have arisen during international negotiations on free trade. The three other countries chosen have specific characteristics that make them interesting from a research perspective. Mexico is geographically close to the United States, but with a different dominant language. Above all, the two countries are linked by a free exchange agreement (NAFTA). Hungary has only been economically "open" since the beginning of the 1990s. South Korea is interesting because it is, a priori, as culturally distant from the United States as it is from Europe. Moreover, it has introduced a protectionist policy in the film sector. The data have been gathered from various organizations (see Table 2). However, we have chosen to use in priority, when available, the data of the European Audiovisual Observatory because, having been reprocessed, they provide a greater guarantee of homogeneity between the data from the different countries in the sample. We should specify that we have treated the European Union as a fictive country whose characteristics are the average of the fifteen member countries,[8] for it is often impossible to group together the data from these countries.[9]

RESULTS

A Greater Variety Supplied and Consumed in the United States, in France, and in the European Union

The variety supplied, at the film level, is estimated on the basis of the number of new full-length films released each year (Table 3) and the number of screens available (Table 4). At the end of the period in question, we can distinguish four groups

---

[8]Nevertheless, the analysis of the situation in the European Union remains incomplete because the data are incomplete or inexistent for Greece, Ireland, Luxembourg, and Portugal. The average is therefore calculated for 13, 14, or 15 countries, depending on the year. We must also specify that the data for the European Union are considered for 15 countries for the whole decade (although Austria, Sweden, and Finland joined later).

[9]For example, the number of new films released in the whole of the European Union is not the sum total of the new films released in each of the 15 member countries (many films are released in every country).

TABLE 1
The Variables Measuring Cultural Diversity in the Film Industry

Analysis Units	Variety		Balance		Disparity	
	Supplied	Consumed	Supplied	Consumed	Supplied	Consumed
Film	Newly released films; Screens/100,000 inhabitants	Admissions per capita	Data unavailable	Market share of top 10 films in total admissions	Methodology unavailable	Methodology unavailable
Genre	Data unavailable	Data unavailable	Data unavailable	Data unavailable	Methodology unavailable	Methodology unavailable
Geographic origin	Data unavailable	Data unavailable	Distribution of newly released films according to 3-D taxonomy	Distribution of admissions according to 3-D taxonomy	Methodology unavailable	Methodology unavailable

TABLE 2
Collected Data

Variables	EU	France	Hungary	Mexico	South Korea	United States
Number of new released films each year	1990–2000 OEA	1990–2000 CNC	1990–2000 OEA	1991–2000[a] Canacine, Tiempo libre	1990–2000 KFO	1990–2000 OEA
Number of screens/100,000 inhabitants	1991–2000 OEA	1990–2000 CNC	1990–2000 OEA	1993–2000 Canacine	1990–2000 KFO	1990–2000 OEA
Admissions per capita	1990–2000 OEA	1990–2000 CNC	1990–2000 OEA	1991–2000[b] Canacine, Tiempo libre	1990–2000 KFO	1990–2000 OEA
Distribution of newly released films according to geographical origin	1990–1999 OEA	1990–2000 CNC	1990–2000 OEA	1991–2000[a,b] Canacine, Tiempo libre	1998–2000 KFO	1995–2000 OEA
Distribution of admissions according to geographical origin	1991–2000 OEA	1990–2000 CNC	1990–2000 NKOM/OEA	1991–2000[a,b] Canacine, Tiempo libre	1998–2000 KFO	1996–2000 OEA
Market share of the top 10 films in total admissions	1996–2000 OEA	1992–2000 CNC	1996–2000 OEA	1999–2000[b] Canacine	1998–2000[c] KFO	1996–2000 OEA/Variety

Note. EU = European Union; OEA = European Audiovisual Observatory; CNC = French National Film Centre; KFO = Korean Film Office; NKOM = Hungarian Ministry of Culture.

[a]Except 1999. [b]Calculated on the basis of data for Mexico City only (the only data available). [c]Calculated on the basis of data for Seoul only (the only data available).

TABLE 3
Number of Films Released in Each Country

Variables	1990	1991	1992	1993	1994	1995	1996	1997	1998	1999	2000
European Union	255	264	247	238	246	261	290	298	298	299	321
France	370	438	392	394	408	405	410	417	470	504	544
Hungary	253	218	190	178	176	143	159	173	165	174	197
Mexico	—	323	311	260	271	290	290	320	296	—	197
South Korea	387	377	415	410	447	423	470	418	333	346	418
United States	385	423	425	440	410	370	420	461	490	442	461

TABLE 4
Number of Screens (for 100,000 Inhabitants)

Variables	1990	1991	1992	1993	1994	1995	1996	1997	1998	1999	2000
European Union	—	4.86	4.79	4.76	4.86	4.99	5.22	5.48	5.82	6.17	6.37
France	7.96	7.78	7.49	7.41	7.43	7.54	7.76	7.95	8.11	8.51	8.61
Hungary	18.19	9.91	6.56	6.16	4.83	5.85	5.47	5.85	6.21	5.67	5.62
Mexico	—	—	—	1.31	1.56	1.64	1.76	1.97	2.20	2.40	2.08
South Korea	1.57	1.76	1.63	1.52	1.41	1.29	1.12	1.08	1.09	1.25	1.54
United States	9.52	9.73	9.83	10.34	10.69	10.57	11.19	11.82	12.65	13.49	13.29

of countries: (a) in France and the United States both the number of new films released and the number of screens are high and increased over the period
1990–2000; (b) in the European Union, the average number of new films released
is lower, as is the number of screens, but the trend over the period is also upward;
(c) in South Korea, although the number of films released is high, it has decreased
since the mid-1990s, and accessibility to these films is low; (d) lastly, in Hungary
and Mexico, few new films are released each year, and the number of screens is
low in Mexico and mediocre in Hungary. In addition, overall the two indicators
have either decreased or risen very weakly in these two countries. In terms of variety supplied, therefore, we see a tendency toward divergence in the performances
of the different countries in the sample. The high performers, the United States,
France, and to a lesser extent the European Union, record a growth in the variety
supplied, whereas the variety supplied in the low performing countries, Mexico
and Hungary, have dropped even further.

Analysis of the variety consumed, based on the level and evolution of average
cinema-going (average number of admissions per inhabitant), leads to relatively
contrasting conclusions (Table 5). In 2000, the United States was the clear leader
in our sample in terms of average cinema-going, ahead of France and the European
Union, with the three other countries recording particularly weak performances.
Analysis of the evolution over the decade 1990–2000 gives quite contrasting observations. The top three countries (United States, France, European Union) are in
a phase of light growth (although average admissions in the United States have
fallen since 1998), whereas the three other countries are in recession (Hungary) or
stagnation (Mexico, South Korea).[10] However, the situation in the last two countries has been improving since 1996.

To sum up, analysis of variety supplied provides the following observation. The
United States, France, and the European Union display a supplied and consumed

---

[10]Of course, the consumption of cultural goods is correlated with per capita gross domestic product
(GDP). It would be interesting to measure the different countries' proclivity for cultural goods by
weighting the volume consumed not only by per capita GDP but also by the price of the goods.

TABLE 5
Admissions Per Capita

Variables	1990	1991	1992	1993	1994	1995	1996	1997	1998	1999	2000
European Union	—	1.65	1.60	1.80	1.83	1.78	1.90	2.05	2.19	2.16	2.25
France	2.15	2.06	2.02	2.30	2.15	2.24	2.34	2.54	2.90	2.62	2.79
Hungary	3.49	2.10	1.47	1.44	1.55	1.38	1.35	1.63	1.44	1.33	1.24
Mexico	—	1.94	1.50	1.13	0.89	0.68	0.86	1.01	1.09	1.24	1.30
South Korea	1.23	1.21	1.08	1.10	1.09	1.01	0.93	1.03	1.08	1.17	1.38
United States	4.78	4.51	4.59	4.82	4.96	4.80	5.05	5.19	5.48	5.32	5.05

variety that is fairly high and tending to rise. South Korea is characterized by an average level of supplied variety (high number of new full-length films but a low number of screens) but a low level of consumed variety. These two indicators have been stagnating over the period as a whole, but with a slight rise since the mid-1990s. Lastly, in Hungary and Mexico, supplied and consumed variety is pretty low and tending to drop over the period as a whole.

A Greater Balance in Terms of Geographical Origin in France, South Korea, and the European Union

The United States appears without any doubt as the country in our sample with the weakest balance in terms of the geographical origin of newly released films. Throughout the decade, they systematically record the highest Herfindhal-Hirschmann index (Table 6).[11] Only about 25% of new releases are nondomestic films.[12] France and the European Union, on the contrary, display the lowest concentrations of films released by geographical origin and therefore the best balanced supply. The supply here is both diversified (about one third of films in each category of origin in France) and stable, or even rising in the case of the European Union (with a fall in the share of American films released and a rise in domestic films). In Hungary and Mexico, on the other hand, the diversity in geographical origin of films released has collapsed, due to a rise in the share of American films and a fall in the share of domestic films. In South Korea, which we could only study over the last three years of the period, the supply in terms of geographical origin is relatively diversified.

Table 7 shows that France had the highest level of consumed diversity, in terms of the balance by geographical origin, throughout the period under investigation.

---

[11]Yet in the case of the United States, the calculation leads to a minimum estimation, because the typology used cannot, by definition, be applied to them. In the case of the United States, the minimum estimation of the HHI is calculated as the square of the national market share.

[12]See the tables in the appendix indicating, for all the countries in the sample, the market shares of national and American films in terms of releases and admissions.

TABLE 6
Herfindhal Hirschmann Index From a Geographical Origin Perspective
(Supply Side)

Variables	1990	1991	1992	1993	1994	1995	1996	1997	1998	1999	2000
European Union	4,170	4,147	3,967	3,979	4,044	3,918	3,931	3,910	3,907	3,755	—
France	3,382	3,345	3,472	3,423	3,369	3,366	3,419	3,465	3,420	3,377	3,415
Hungary	4,045	4,371	4,045	4,855	4,848	5,370	4,668	5,246	5,154	5,112	4,703
Mexico	—	3,917	4,123	4,696	4,270	4,346	5,296	5,684	5,457	—	5,499
South Korea	—	—	—	—	—	—	—	—	4,473	4,468	4,005
United States[a]	—	—	—	—	—	5,933	6,553	7,416	7,001	5,642	5,601

[a]Minimal value calculated considering only domestic films' market share.

TABLE 7
Herfindhal Hirschmann Index From a Geographical Origin Perspective
(Demand Side)

Variables	1990	1991	1992	1993	1994	1995	1996	1997	1998	1999	2000
European Union	—	5,718	5,718	5,950	5,822	5,584	5,502	4,878	6,234	5,246	5,874
France	4,575	4,431	4,651	4,557	4,631	4,267	4,424	4,091	4,844	4,144	4,772
Hungary	4,088	4,583	4,394	5,150	8,935	8,329	7,933	6,305	8,384	6,636	7,418
Mexico	—	—	—	—	—	6,792	8,072	8,246	8,577	7,459[a]	7,635[a]
South Korea	—	—	—	—	—	—	—	—	5,735	4,514	4,259
United States[b]	—	—	—	—	—	—	9,160	8,529	8,959	8,305	8,560

[a]Over-estimated data based on the hypothesis that U.S. films' market share is equal to 100% minus domestic films' market share. [b]Minimal value calculated considering only domestic films' market share.

Moreover, its situation is relatively stable, with a market share for domestic films amongst the highest in the study (excepting the United States) at around 30% —although this falls slightly over the decade—and a constant market share for American films of around 60%. However, in 2000, France was overtaken by South Korea, where domestic films as well as "other films" enjoyed greater success in the cinemas. The European Union displays weaker consumed balance by origin but equally stable over the period as a whole: a market share of 20% for domestic films (showing slight growth over the decade)[13] and a market share for American films just above 70%. In Hungary, the balance of admissions in terms of origin deteriorated sharply from its particularly high level at the start of the decade, thanks to a market share of "other films" oscillating around the 40% mark. The HHI at the end

---

[13]However, attention should be paid to the procedure used for recording the nationality of EU films. Certain countries record any production in which they have participated as national, even if they have only been a minority coproducer.

of the period was thus very high, notably due to the growth in market share of U.S. films. The same is true for Mexico, which only managed 13.7% of admissions for Mexican films in 2000, although even this compares favorably with the 1.5% recorded in 1998! Lastly, consumed diversity by geographical origin is weakest in the United States: more than 90% of admissions were for domestic films. Overall, there is an important trend toward dualism in admissions between domestic and American films (since 1995, no country has recorded a market share for "other films" exceeding 15%). Over the whole period, Mexico and the United States recorded weak levels of consumed diversity by origin, although there was a slight improvement toward the end of the decade. In Hungary, the situation deteriorated from the start of the decade to reach a very weak balance at the end. In France and the European Union, the situation remained globally stable over the whole period, while in South Korea it improved dramatically.

Degree of Concentration of Admissions on a Small Number of Films

Comparison of balance between the different countries in the sample in terms of individual films has been rendered difficult by a lack of precision in the data. The share in total admissions of the top 10 films can only be calculated from 1996 onward (1992 for France), and even 1999 for Mexico and 1998 for South Korea[14] (Table 8).

The CR_{10} criterion makes little distinction between the different countries. Over the period 1998–2000, the top 10 films obtained on average more than 25% of admissions in all the countries in the sample. However, the concentration of admissions on a small number of films appears to be higher in France and in South Korea and, on the contrary, lower in the European Union as a whole and in the United States. Hungary and Mexico occupy intermediate positions. Evolution of this criterion over the decade appears to be quite erratic for all the countries. France, the only country for which a long series of data is available, records an upward trend.[15, 16] Thus, if cinema-going in France during the period 1990–2000 has increased, this rise has essentially been to the benefit of a small number of big successes. The network effect that characterizes film consump-

---

[14]In these last two countries, the calculation has only been made for the cities of Mexico and Seoul.

[15]Except for the two peaks due to the release of the films *Les Visiteurs* in 1993 and *Titanic* in 1998.

[16]Of course, it would be interesting to counterbalance this analysis with an analysis of the balance of individual films on the supply side, for example, by analyzing the top 10 films' share (in number of prints) of the total number of prints released. Unfortunately, such analysis is impossible at this time.

[17]Cultural consumption is characterized by network externalities arising from phenomena of mimicry and social infectiousness. To reduce their uncertainty about the quality of cultural products, most consumers tend to consume the products they have heard about (from friends, press, or publicity) or which achieve the most commercial success. On this question, see Kretschmer, Klimis, and Choi (1999).

TABLE 8
CR_{10} (Demand Side)

Variables	1990	1991	1992	1993	1994	1995	1996	1997	1998	1999	2000
European Union	—	—	—	—	—	—	25.0	23.9	27.3	27.4	21.9
France	—	—	27.1	34.0	29.8	24.2	27.4	28.8	39.5	30.5	29.5
Hungary	—	—	—	—	—	—	27.1	27.8	29.3	32.3	29.3
Mexico	—	—	—	—	—	—	—	—	—	29.8	27.4
South Korea	—	—	—	—	—	—	—	—	33.3	42.4	35.3
United States	—	—	—	—	—	—	28.0	23.6	27.3	27.9	22.2

tion,[17] accentuated by the supply strategies of the producers (investments in notoriety) and the distributors (the number of copies put into circulation), thus seems to result in a concentration of admissions on a limited number of films, to the detriment of cultural diversity.

Links Between Supplied Diversity and Consumed Diversity

Analysis of the links between supplied diversity and consumed diversity leads to two observations. On one hand, in every country, supplied diversity by geographical origin is always greater than consumed diversity.[18] This seems to be due to the production strategy of the culture industries (see preceding discussion). A large number of works are produced in order to minimize the risks by compensating for the (numerous) failures by the (rare) successes. We should, however, note that the market share in admissions obtained by American films is always greater than their market share in distribution. Is this because the consumers in every country in the sample have an intrinsic preference for U.S. films or because of the strategies used by the producers and distributors of these films? Further analyses would have to be carried out in order to answer this question.

On the other hand, there is a strong positive correlation between consumed diversity by origin and supplied diversity by origin.[19] In other words, consumed diversity can only reach a high level in countries where supplied diversity is also high. To be more precise, there is a strong positive correlation between the share of domestic films in distribution and their share in receipts[20] as there is between the

---

[18]Over the 11 years and for the six countries, we have 39 observations of the comparative level of the HHI by origin for the supply and the HHI by origin for the consumption. The average index of the supply is 4,222 and that of the consumption is 5,782.

[19]Over the 39 observations of the comparative level of the HHI by origin for supply and the HHI by origin for consumption, the coefficient of correlation is 0.82.

[20]Over the 52 possible observations of the market share of domestic films in distribution and receipts respectively, the coefficient of correlation between these two variables is 0.95 (but only 0.82 if the United States is left out of the sample).

share of American films in distribution and their share in receipts.[21] This observation seems to confirm the nature of the market for the supply of cultural goods and services. Because of the uncertainty of success, it is the demand that adapts to the supply and not the other way round. Thus, demand for diversity could end up being stifled by a standardized supply. An active policy of growth in supplied diversity is liable to result in growth of the demand for diversity. Thus, if France records the best performances over the decade in terms of the market share in admissions of domestic films (33% on average over the period 1990–2000), this is clearly due to the share they obtain in distribution (37.6% on average over the period). We must, however, underline the fact that South Korea represents an exception to the rule. This country saw the market share in admissions of domestic productions grow considerably (from 20.2% in 1990 to 32.6% in 2000) while their share in distribution fell (28.7% in 1990 compared with 14.1% in 2000).

DISCUSSION

Some Comments on the Results

Table 9, which summarizes all the data collected in the form of averages over the period 1990–2000 taken as a whole (or a shorter period when data were unavailable), enables us to sketch out a multicriteria classification of the six countries in terms of cultural diversity in the film industry. This multicriteria analysis notably highlights the differences in ranking that appear as a function of the different meanings given to cultural diversity.

Mexico, and to a lesser extent Hungary, display weak performances for all the criteria used and can thus be ranked in the last two places. The classification of the other four countries, on the other hand, depends on whether more importance is attached to the variables representing variety (released films, screens, admissions) or to the variables representing balance (supplied HHI, consumed HHI, CR_{10}). If variety is considered to be more important, the United States and France perform best, ahead of the European Union and South Korea. If, on the contrary, more importance is attached to balance, then it is France and the European Union that lead the field, followed by South Korea and, far behind, the United States. If we take all the criteria equally into consideration, the ranking for cultural diversity in the film industry could be as follows. In first place, France, which achieves good performances for both types of variable (variety and balance), followed by the European Union, the performances of which are similar but systematically lower (except for the CR_{10}). The third place is shared by the United States and South Korea. The to-

---

[21]Over the 38 possible observations of the market share of American films in distribution and receipts respectively, the coefficient of correlation between these two variables is 0.78.

TABLE 9
Average Values of Variables Over the Period 1990 to 2000

	Variety			Balance		
	Supplied		Consumed	Supplied by Origin	Consumed by Origin	Consumed by Film
Variables	Released Films	Screens	Admissions Per Capita	Supplied HHI	Consumed HHI	CR_{10}
European Union	304.0	6.0	2.2	3,857.3	5,558.0	25.1
France	483.8	8.3	2.7	3,419.3	4,462.8	32.1
Hungary	177.3	5.8	1.4	5,053.8	7,185.8	29.7
Mexico	271.0	2.2	1.2	5,546.7	8,411.5	28.6
South Korea	378.8	1.2	1.2	4,315.3	4,836.0	37.0
United States	463.5	12.8	5.3	6,415.0	8,588.3	25.3

Note.   HHI = Herfindhal–Hirschmann index.

tally opposite profiles of these two countries make it impossible to decide between them. In the United States cultural diversity seems to be expressed by variety, whereas in South Korea it has more to do with balance in terms of geographical origin. More films are released in the United States than in South Korea, the United States has 10 times more screens per capita than South Korea, and Americans go to the cinema four times more often than South Koreans, almost certainly revealing a strong inequality in access to cultural consumption in South Korea. On the other hand, supplied and consumed diversity in terms of geographical origin in South Korea is among the highest in the sample, while the United States is ranked in sixth place for this criterion. Lastly, in fifth and sixth places, come Hungary and Mexico. Furthermore, calculations (not shown here) demonstrate that the average performances over the last three years are almost always higher than the average performances over the whole decade for the European Union, the United States, and, to a lesser extent, France, whereas they are lower for Hungary and Mexico.[22] Thus, the current gaps between the different countries in the sample in terms of cultural diversity seem to be widening rather than closing.

As we have just highlighted, the diagnosis of supplied and consumed cultural diversity in a country depends heavily on the dimensions chosen (only variety, only balance, or the two together). According to us, of course, and according to the theoretic works dedicated to economic analysis of diversity (see previous discussion), the multidimensional approach should be chosen. Furthermore, this opposition between single-dimensional and multidimensional approaches seems to explain the antagonisms between the position of certain states (notably France and

---

[22]The data on South Korea at the beginning of the decade are too fragmented to give any significance to this comparison.

Canada) and the position adopted by the large cultural industry groups as regards cultural diversity. Thus Jean-Marie Messier, the ex-CEO of Vivendi Universal, pointed to the rise in the volume of cultural production (film, music, and publishing), the growth in consumption and the (relative) success of domestic productions in the cultural consumption of each country as proof that cultural diversity is thriving.[23] If we restrict ourselves to these criteria, cultural diversity does indeed seem to be in a healthy state, but in reality it is threatened by the concentration of consumption on a small number of films and by the low diversity on the screens and in admissions in terms of geographical origin.

Toward an Analysis of the Determining Factors of Cultural Diversity

The tool for measuring cultural diversity presented in this article could be used to test different hypotheses concerning the possible determining factors of cultural diversity. Without making any claim for completeness, for this raises quite another subject of research, it is nevertheless possible to envisage the testing of the following relations.

Diversity and concentration. The link between industrial concentration and diversity is ambiguous, to say the least. If too much concentration is undoubtedly harmful to diversity, it also appears that too much competition leads firms to adopt strategies of mimicry that are hardly propitious to cultural diversity. According to Van der Wurff and Van Cuilenburg (2001), three scenarios are possible: fierce competition tending to reduce prices and diversity, moderate competition that maintains prices at a higher level but with more diversity, or collusion resulting in high prices and low diversity. It would therefore be useful to be able to evaluate, in terms of industries (extending to other areas and not just the film industry) and countries, the nature of the competition that predominates and its consequences for cultural diversity.

Diversity and promotional strategies. At this time we can observe a tendency toward the standardization of production (a fall in disparity) together with a tendency toward concentration of promotion (in the widest sense of the term, namely production budget, marketing, number of copies in circulation, etc.) on a small number of products, even if the actual number of new products remains high. In other words, more and more products have an extremely short life, which does not give them the time to "meet" their demand. It would then be a question of testing the impact on consumed diversity of strategies tending to increase the appearance of vari-

---

[23]*Le Monde,* April 9, 2001.

ety by the growth in new products while reducing the accessibility of most of them. Some results of this article clearly illustrate this topic. Hence, although the share of French films in distribution tended to increase over the decade, their share in admissions tended to fall to the benefit of "other" films and above all American films, despite the fact that the share of American films in distribution fell over the same period. This fall was probably compensated for by a strategy of increasing the number of copies in circulation, making it possible to obtain a better rate of screen occupation with a smaller number of films. Another cause for concern is the trend toward concentration of admissions on the top 10 films of the year (see Table 8). Here again, a detailed analysis of distribution and promotion strategies, for both French and American films, could help to explain these developments.

Diversity and vertical integration.   The case of Hungarian cinema suggests that the adoption of strategies of vertical integration by the large communication groups toward the sectors of distribution and broadcasting has considerable consequences in terms of diversity. Several phenomena may explain the strong growth in the distribution and admissions of American films in Hungary. First, distribution in Hungary is currently dominated by a duopoly formed by Intercom and UIP Danube.[24] Now, UIP Danube is a joint venture between Paramount and Universal. And Intercom, which also possesses the biggest network of cinemas in the country, has signed long-term distribution agreements with several Hollywood studios (Warner, Columbia-Tristar, Fox, and Disney). Second, there has been a real craze for multiplex cinemas in Hungary over the last few years (there are now 12, which between them account for half of admission receipts) and most of them are owned by Intercom. So it appears that everything is ready to provide American films, distributed in ever greater numbers in Hungary, with privileged distribution.

Diversity and public policy.   The tools for measuring cultural diversity proposed in this article could be used as the basis for analyzing the respective influences of different instruments of public policy (quotas, support for production, etc.) on diversity, and not just on the protection of the national cultural industries. At first glance, protectionism indeed seems to favor diversity in an industry where American movies are often hegemonic. Hence, it seems unlikely that the ranking of France, the European Union, and South Korea, countries in which systems of support for the domestic film industry exist, is pure coincidence. However, it is not at all certain that a protectionist policy based on quotas for the production or distribution of domestic films always achieves greater cultural diversity. If such policies result simply in the substitution of American films, which are predominant in every country in the sample, by domestic films, to the detriment of "other films," the

---

[24]*Actualités internationales*, CNC, No. 201, April 2002.

objective of increasing cultural diversity will not be achieved. Moreover, even if today, despite the fall in domestic production, South Korean films seem to be winning ever more favor with the public (see Table D in the appendix), there is another side to the coin. This new growth is essentially to the benefit of films inspired by Hollywood formulas and video game scenarios.

REFERENCES

Anderson, C. L. (1992). Canadian content laws and programming diversity. *Canadian Public Policy, 18*, 166–175.

Caves, R. E. (2000). *Creative industries.* Cambridge, MA: Harvard University Press.

Cohendet, P., Llerena, P., & Sorge, A. (1992). Technological diversity and coherence in Europe: An analytical overview. *Revue d'Economie Industrielle, 59*, 9–26.

Frenken, K., Saviotti, P. P., & Trommetter, M. (1999). Variety and niche creation in aircraft, helicopters, motorcycles and microcomputers. *Research Policy, 28*, 469–488.

Iosifidis, P. (1999). Diversity versus concentration in the deregulated mass media domain. *Journalism and Mass Communication Quarterly, 76*, 152–162.

Kogut, B., & Singh, H. (1988). The effect of the national culture on the choice of entry mode. *Journal of International Business Studies, 19*(3), 411–432.

Kretschmer, M., Klimis, G. M., & Choi, C. J. (1999). Increasing returns and social contagion in cultural industries. *British Journal of Management, 10*, S61–S72.

Metrick, A., & Weitzman, M. L. (1998). Conflicts and choices in biodiversity preservation. *Journal of Economic Perspectives, 12*, 21–34.

Sarrina Li, S. C., & Chiang, C. C. (2001). Market competition and programming diversity: A study on the TV market in Taiwan. *Journal of Media Economics, 14*, 105–120.

Saviotti, P. P. (1996). *Technological evolution, variety and the economy.* Cheltenham: Edward Elgar.

Solow, A., Polasky, S., & Broadus, J. (1993). On the measurement of biological diversity. *Journal of Environmental Economics and Management, 24*, 60–68.

Stirling, A. (1999). On the economics and analysis of diversity. *SPRU Electronic Working Paper, no.* 28.

Van der Wurff, R. (2002). Competition and diversity in European broadcasting, 12th International Conference on Cultural Economics, Rotterdam, June 2002.

Van der Wurff, R., & Van Cuilenburg, J. (2001). Impact of moderate and ruinous competition on diversity: The Dutch television market. *Journal of Media Economics, 14*, 213–229.

Weitzman, M. L. (1992). On diversity. *Quarterly Journal of Economics, 107*, 363–406.

Weitzman, M. L. (1993). What to preserve? An application of diversity to crane conservation. *Quarterly Journal of Economics, 102*, 157–183.

Weitzman, M. L. (2000). Economic profitability versus ecological entropy. *Quarterly Journal of Economics, 109*, 237–263.

APPENDIX

TABLE A
Market Share of Domestic Films on the Supply Side (%)

Variables	1990	1991	1992	1993	1994	1995	1996	1997	1998	1999	2000
European Union	12.7	13.6	15.0	15.7	14.7	15.1	15.8	15.4	15.4	17.4	—
France	34.9	32.0	42.6	39.3	35.8	36.8	39.3	40.8	37.4	36.3	38.2
Hungary	12.3	8.7	13.2	10.7	11.4	6.3	12.6	9.2	7.9	9.2	9.6
Mexico	—	27.2	22.2	18.8	19.9	13.8	6.9	6.3	2.7	—	8.1
South Korea	28.7	32.1	23.1	15.4	14.5	15.1	13.8	14.1	12.9	14.2	14.1
United States	—	—	—	—	—	77.0	81.0	86.1	83.7	75.1	74.8

TABLE B
Market Share of U.S. Firms on the Supply Side (%)

Variables	1990	1991	1992	1993	1994	1995	1996	1997	1998	1999	2000
European Union	53.6	54.0	50.5	51.6	52.4	49.0	50.3	49.2	49.0	45.9	—
France	37.3	36.1	30.9	34.5	35.8	34.3	34.4	34.5	36.8	35.7	35.7
Hungary	48.6	53.7	50.5	64.0	64.2	68.5	62.3	68.2	66.7	66.7	61.4
Mexico	—	52.6	56.3	63.5	58.3	57.9	67.9	71.9	67.6	—	70.6
South Korea	—	—	—	—	—	—	—	—	59.6	60.0	50.6

TABLE C
Domestic Films Market Share in Admissions

Variables	1990	1991	1992	1993	1994	1995	1996	1997	1998	1999	2000
European Union	—	17.0	17.0	15.0	15.0	16.0	19.0	22.0	16.0	17.0	23.0
France	37.5	30.6	34.9	35.1	28.3	35.2	37.5	34.5	27.3	32.4	28.5
Hungary	12.0	5.2	7.0	8.1	0.8	1.0	5.3	9.2	3.0	5.7	4.5
Mexico	—	—	—	—	—	6.1	3.5	2.4	1.5	14.3	13.7
South Korea	20.2	21.2	18.5	15.9	20.5	20.9	23.1	25.5	21.3	35.8	32.6
United States	—	—	—	—	—	—	95.7	92.4	94.7	91.1	92.5

TABLE D
U.S. Films' Market Share in Admissions

Variables	1990	1991	1992	1993	1994	1995	1996	1997	1998	1999	2000
European Union	—	73.0	73.0	75.0	74.0	72.0	71.0	65.0	77.0	69.0	73.0
France	55.9	58.0	58.2	57.1	60.9	53.9	54.3	52.2	63.3	53.9	62.2
Hungary	50.0	53.0	49.7	66.7	94.4	90.9	88.7	77.8	91.3	80.0	85.4
Mexico	—	—	—	—	—	81.2	89.5	90.5	92.4	—	—
South Korea	—	—	—	—	—	—	—	—	72.4	56.3	55.2

Broadcast Network Television, 1955–2003: The Pursuit of Advertising and the Decline of Diversity

Mara Einstein
Department of Media Studies
Queens College

Over the past 30 years, scholars have turned to economic models to analyze diversity in the media marketplace (De Jong & Bates, 1991; Dominick & Pearce, 1976; Entman & Wildman, 1992; Grant, 1994; Litman, 1979; van der Wurff & van Cuilenburg, 2001). In using these methodologies, the overwhelming conclusion is that diversity is declining. In particular, the traditional broadcast networks (ABC, CBS, and NBC) have seen steady erosion in viewer options.

Trying to find a reason for this decline has been difficult, though scholars attempt to draw conclusions between the suppliers of programming and the types of programs produced (Beebe, 1977; Einstein, 2004; Levin, 1971), that is, source diversity, or between the number of outlets and the types of programs produced (Chan-Olmsted, 1996; Grant, 1994; Li & Chiang, 2001; Owen, 1978), that is, outlet diversity.

Intuitively, increasing the number of people creating programming should increase the types of programming produced. Similarly, providing producers with more channels for their programming should create additional opportunities for creating a variety of options for viewers. However, in study after study, this has not been the case. Napoli (1999), after reviewing a plethora of diversity studies, concludes that there has been no definitive relationship established between source diversity and the programming produced. As for outlet diversity, researchers (De Jong & Bates, 1991; Le Duc, 1982) explain that increasing the number of services does not necessarily increase diversity, because new outlets often offer the same types of programs as established ones. Research in audience behavior also indi-

Requests for reprints should be sent to Mara Einstein, Department of Media Studies, Queens College, 65–30 Kissena Blvd., Flushing, NY 11367. E-mail: drmeinstein@hotmail.com

cates that increasing the number of outlets may not be the means to increasing the diversity of messages for viewers, because viewers do not necessarily opt to watch the incremental choices available to them (Webster & Phalen, 1994; Wober, 1989). Moreover, and I would add more importantly, the economic structure does not lend itself to diversity. Curran (1991) states that "market structures determine and impose limits on ... 'diversity.' ... This means ... [among other things] constraints imposed by catering for the mass market" (p. 94).

Reliance on advertising, which dictates catering to a mass audience, constitutes a constraint on the diversity of programming. Because of this economic model, television producers need to create programming that works within limited, formulaic guidelines that depend on recognizable characters, themes, and subject matter (Herskovitz, 1997, p. 187) and that cater to advertiser-desirable audiences. In addition, programming over time has been forced to appeal to smaller and smaller audience segments to achieve bigger and bigger profits. As Grant (1994) states, "Many media outlets maximize their profit by targeting smaller 'high-value' audiences rather than mass audiences, taking advantage of the fact that advertisers place greater value on their potential return from the audience members reached than on the sheer number of audience members" (p. 52).

This research will attempt to demonstrate that changes in the advertising environment—specifically changes in the early 1960s when advertising moved from total show sponsorship to spot participation, the widespread acceptance of selling based on demographics in the 1970s, and the advent of cable and other competitors starting in the 1980s–have caused broadcast network programming to become less diverse.

METHOD

Diversity of broadcast network program content in prime time was measured from 1955 until the present. The three major broadcast networks (ABC, CBS, and NBC) were evaluated because they were the only programming that was available to all U.S. television households throughout the period being studied, and this programming allows for understanding a changing advertising marketplace and its effect on diversity. The beginning period was selected as this is the point at which television had reached 50% penetration of American homes. Prime time (8 p.m. to 11 p.m. Monday through Saturday and 7 p.m. to 11 p.m. Sunday) was the period studied because it is when most viewers watch, it receives the majority of program spending (39%), and it contributes the majority of profits (Media Dynamics, 1998, p. 41). During the early years studied, the three major networks accounted for more than 90% of viewing during prime time hours. Although that number is significantly less than that more recently (usually in the range from 45%–50%), these networks still account for the lion's share of television viewing.

The Herfindahl-Hirschman Index (HHI) was used to analyze program concentration. This index measures vertical diversity, that is, the level of concentration of programming within genres throughout the entire schedule. The HHI is an index used by economists to measure concentration in an industry. Media scholars have adapted it to determine diversity in program content. The benefit of using this index over others is that it more heavily weights the largest areas of concentration. For example, if six program types represented 15% each of the program schedule and all other programming represented 1%, the HHI would be 1,360, considered to be moderately concentrated. However, if one genre represented 70% of programming while two others were 10%, and all other programming was 1%, the HHI would be 5,110—well over the level considered to be concentrated according to the Department of Justice guidelines, which will be discussed more fully in the following section. This example demonstrates how, if one genre of programming becomes particularly popular, it will be evident with this index.

In evaluating the content of programming, determining an appropriate taxonomy that is relevant throughout the decades studied is a particular stumbling block. The 1960s were full of musical and comedy/variety series, whereas the 1990s and 2000s have "reality" series. This includes shows such as *Survivor* or *The Bachelor* or *America's Funniest Home Videos*, which were unheard of in previous decades. Elsewhere I have evaluated similar programming with two different taxonomies—one that provided a better fit with programming from the earlier time period and one created to more appropriately fit programming in the more recent time period. The difference between the two codes was negligible (Einstein, 2004). Therefore, for this study, categorizations fitting the earlier time period were used, because they applied more closely to programming throughout the period studied. This taxonomy was from a study by L. W. Lichty, who evaluated programming from 1949 through 1973 (Sterling & Kittross, 1978, p. 528–531). Previous researchers have used a variety of program categories ranging from 5 to 15 (Dominick & Pearce, 1976; Steiner, 1963; Wildman & Robinson, 1995). This research uses 22 categories. Although this number is larger than that used by other researchers, it is possible that the existing level of diversity may not be captured.

Program schedules were from McNeil (1996) for the period from 1955 until 1995. Schedules from subsequent years were from *Broadcasting and Cable* and *Variety,* major industry trade publications. Only regularly scheduled programming was considered, eliminating specials from this analysis. Movies were grouped together, because any more fine-grained distinctions would require a special study. Shows were categorized based on descriptions in McNeil and in later years from zap2it.com (and its predecessor ultimatetv.com), a Web site that includes show descriptions and press releases containing descriptions of television programs, as well as network and program distributor Web sites.

Time, rather than shows, was used as the basic unit for analysis. This was to account for the variety in show lengths in the 1950s, 1960s, and 1970s. Some shows were 45 min, some 90 min, in addition to the 30 or 60 min shows we are used to to-day. Therefore, quarter hours were used as the time period of analysis. More programming was evaluated in the seasons prior to 1971. After 1971, program hours in prime time were reduced significantly due to the introduction of the Prime Time Access Rule.

DIVERSITY ANALYSIS

The HHI has been used by scholars to evaluate diversity of the media (Greco, 1999; Litman, 1979; Park, 1999). This index measures diversity by taking into account all programming on the schedule. The HHI is calculated by summing the squares of the percentage, or share, of each program type. This index measures "the size distribution of programming. ... The higher the Herfindahl index, the greater the concentration of programming into a few program types, and hence the less the diversity" (Litman, 1979, p. 403). Thus if we can equate high concentration with a limited number of program types and an inequality in size, then we can use this index as a determinant of lack of diversity.

In looking at Figure 1, we see that diversity fluctuates between 910 and 1,918. According to the Department of Justice, which uses the HHI in determining if a merger is anticompetitive, an industry is in one of three categories: "(a)

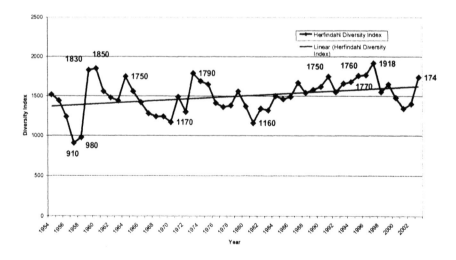

FIGURE 1   Diversity of prime time programming, Big 3 broadcast networks, 1954–2003.

unconcentrated (HHI below 1,000), (b) moderately concentrated (HHI between 1,000 and 1,800), and (c) highly concentrated (HHI above 1,800)" (Greco, 1999). Therefore, according to this guideline, 1957 and 1958 (HHI 910 and 980, respectively) are the only points in which diversity is below what is considered to be a concentrated level. Throughout the rest of the period studied, the diversity index is in the moderately concentrated range of 1,000 to 1,800. The index has been near or above the concentrated level nine times with the majority of these concentration points occurring in the past 10 years. The most concentrated years were 1959, 1960, 1973, and 1997 (1,830, 1,850, 1,790, and 1,918, respectively). As the trend line suggests, there is a steadily decreasing level of diversity away from moderate concentration to full-scale concentration in program content.

CHANGES IN DIVERSITY

High Diversity—New Medium

The high level of diversity in the 1950s can be attributed to the development of new genres as this nascent industry grew. In television's infancy, networks relied on programming that was developed from radio formats, such as musical and variety shows. By the mid-1950s, producers began to develop programming that was more visual and better suited to the medium. This included westerns and crime/detective series. At diversity's peak, therefore, the medium provided a more equitable blend of the older radio-transferred programs combined with new programming. As the medium progressed, visually oriented programming became more dominant on the schedule, while radio formats began to disappear, and diversity began to decline.

Low Diversity—Advertiser dependence

The periods of least diversity can be accounted for in a number of ways. In the late 1950s, two key issues affected diversity—the means by which programs were selected and the means by which programming was sold to advertisers—two issues that are indelibly interrelated. Prior to the 1960s, advertisers, independent producers and the networks were all part of the prime time selection process. Revenue was generated through advertisers paying for time periods with complete packages of shows and advertising, that is, fully sponsored programming.

After the quiz show scandals of the late 1950s and because of the increased cost of producing television programming, broadcasters took over responsibility for selecting programming, and single sponsorship virtually disappeared. Single sponsorship declined from 39.5% to 10.3% between 1957 and 1964 (Amendment of Part 73, 1965, p. 2168). Ultimately that number would drop even further, so that by 1968 less than 4% of prime-time programming was supplied directly by advertisers (Amendment of Part 73, 1970, p. 390). Thus, by the end of the 1960s, the majority of programming was being sold to advertisers as spot participation and not as full sponsorships. Because networks now had to prove their value to advertisers by producing ratings, they needed to guarantee as best they could that they would produce a large audience. Thus, the most popular programming becomes readily duplicated, as was the case with westerns and crime programming in the late 1950s.

There is precedence for this in radio as suggested by Dimmick and McDonald (2001) in their study on network radio. They conclude that

> Power was dispersed over a disparate group of decision-makers such as advertising agencies, the networks, and independent suppliers as well as radio "stars." As a result of the practice of full sponsorship, radio programs were not aimed at the same mass audience but instead were targeted at the audience segment that was believed to be the potential buyers for the product sponsoring the program. (p. 209)

Once television decision making was put into the hands of the networks (instead of multiple decision makers as in radio), programming became less diverse because the broadcast networks were working to optimize profit, which perforce meant catering to large audiences in order to attract the most money from advertisers. Whether it was the gatekeeping properties of the networks or the means of advertising sales that had a larger effect on diversity is impossible to say.

Low Diversity—Regulation and Deregulation

The declining diversity in 1973 and in 1997 can at least in part be attributed to regulation and deregulation respectively. In the late 1960s, the government was concerned about violence in programming. Much of that violence occurred in action/adventure programming and westerns, which had been a staple of prime-time programming throughout the 1950s and early 1960s. In response, the networks moved away from this type of programming. By 1973, there were no adventure programs, whereas there had been 14 hours per week only 6 years before. Similarly, there were only 2 hours of western programming where as there had been more than 13 hours of westerns 6 years before. These genres, which were much more sedate than similar programming today, were reduced or eliminated in deference to the crime category, which in the same time period grew from 5.5 hours to more than 16 hours a week. Alternatively, in 1995, the financial interest and syndication rules were repealed allowing the networks to now own and syndicate programming that appeared on their air. Situation comedies have traditionally been the most lucrative shows in syndication, and in 1997 there were a record 40 situation comedies in prime time, representing 30% of prime-time programming.

Declining Diversity—Demographics, Structural Changes, and the Fight for Ad Dollars

The 1970s introduced the period wherein the networks began to compete for audiences based on demographic targets. In the mid-1950s, less than 10% of network television was sold based on demographics. By the mid-1970s, more than 80% of television was bought by advertisers using this methodology, with 55% of buys targeting adults 18 to 49 years of age and 20% targeting adults 25 to 54 (Media Dynamics, 1998, p. 82). Thus, programming was created to appeal to these target audiences, and through the mid-1970s diversity declined. However, by 1976, that trend changed. Litman (1979) suggests that the increase in diversity in the latter part of the 1970s occurred due to ABC's rise from third to first place. Traditionally, ABC had a weaker affiliate group and poor relationships with the Hollywood creative community. Because of their last place standing, the network was able to take more chances, and in 1976 "ABC began a new trend toward nostalgia, sex appeal, and double entendre comedy ... [which] struck such a resonant chord with young influential viewers that ABC soon became the number one network" (p. 397). This diversity increase would be short-lived, however, because the other networks would copy their strategy and thus reduce diversity. This scenario—last place network takes a risk with programming and rival networks quickly follow suit—would be repeated throughout television's history. Most recently this was seen with the plethora of game shows and reality series. More important at the time, however, would be the introduction of new competitors.

The 1980s saw tremendous structural changes in the television industry, most notably the introduction of a fourth broadcast network, Fox, and the increasing penetration of cable, both basic and premium channels. No longer were the Big Three competing against just each other, but also with a younger-skewing broadcaster and a plethora of cable networks that offered programming that had once been the exclusive staple of the more established networks.

These new competitors forced the networks to become more targeted, and thus less diverse, in order to maximize profits. This was true for two reasons—greater competition for ad dollars and smaller, more defined audiences for whom to create programming. Cable increased competition for ad dollars because this new medium did not increase overall spending. Rather, advertisers were moving money from their television buy, which meant broadcast, and putting it into cable. By 1990, cable had made significant inroads. That year, cable ad sales more than doubled from 1985, while broadcast sales grew by only 16% over the same period (Media Dynamics, 1998). Over the course of the 1990s, cable network advertising would grow to 8.3 billion dollars, growing at a rate of approximately 20% a year. At the same time, broadcast network advertising sales (including Fox, UPN, and the WB) would reach 14.6 billion dollars at a rate of 3% (PricewaterhouseCoopers, 2000). Because advertisers had another medium on which to spend their money, the established networks became risk averse, which translates into less diverse programming.

Cable also solidified the need to attract finely tuned demographic targets. Cable became profitable by targeting very specific demographics. For example, MTV targets teens, for which advertisers are willing to pay a hefty premium. As network shares declined due to erosion from cable and later Direct Broadcast Satellite (DBS), the established networks, too, had to more narrowly define their audiences. The networks have done this to varying degrees and levels of success: ABC targets families, CBS targets adults 25–54, and NBC targets adults 18–49 with household incomes of $75,000. The recent upfront market—the time period when networks sell 75% to 80% of their inventory—provides an example of why these demographics are so important. While CBS was the leader in household ratings and the older 25–54 demographic, the network received $2.2 billion. NBC, the leader in the advertiser-coveted 18–49 demographic, got $3 billion out of a total $9.3 billion market (McCarthy, 2003). Attracting this young adult target is mandatory for achieving profitably and why CBS is trying to target younger and younger audiences.

Taken to the extreme, the broadcast networks over time are likely to become more like cable networks. We can see a glimpse of this in the summer programming that broadcasters provide. Historically during the summer, the broadcast networks have offered reruns of their regular schedule. Viewers would sample cable fare because they knew they would not see anything new on the networks. The cable networks took on the strategy of introducing new programming during the summer so as not to compete with broadcasters. For the first time in the summer of 2003, the broadcast networks have scheduled original programming in order to be competitive. They have all targeted young adults in their programming with primarily reality programming and newsmagazines, which are relatively inexpensive to produce vis-à-vis scripted shows and provide incremental revenue sources (Levine & Fass, 2003).

As is evident from Figure 2, when the broadcast networks compete on costs, they no longer compete on programming. Virtually identical programming appears on all the networks, which is seen by the very high Herfindahl index. In fact these numbers are so concentrated as to be well above what the Department of Justice considers to be anticompetitive.

At this extreme, what we are seeing is what van Cuilenburg in 1999 called "ruinous competition." In this situation

> Broadcasters will start replacing cost leadership strategies with short-term price competition strategies to minimize first copy costs. They will offer low quality content at low prices. Audiences will turn to other media markets and revenues will decline further. The end result will be that the remaining broadcasters all offer the same content. (van der Wurff & van Cuilenburg, 2001, p. 216)

Herfindahl Index - Summer 2003

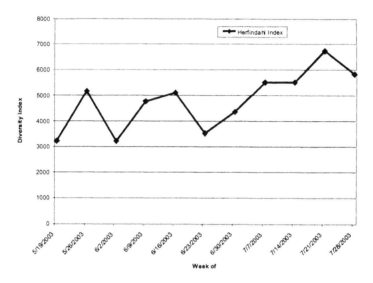

FIGURE 2   Broadcast network prime time diversity index, summer 2003.

Viewers turn to cable because of the lack of diversity on the networks. I would add to this that ruinous competition occurs because broadcasters are all targeting the same market, not just trying to create large audiences.

CONCLUSION AND DISCUSSION

In studying diversity for more than 30 years, scholars have on the whole determined that diversity is decreasing. Even with the introduction of new programming outlets, such as cable and DBS, there are still no new forms of programming available for the viewing public. While there may be horizontal diversity with the added number of channels, vertical diversity—as has been argued by other scholars—has not been achieved.

In part this may be a fault of the methodology. The limits of the scales being used to assess diversity do little to inform us of whether there is truly a multiplicity of viewpoints. For example, although *All in the Family* and *Suddenly Susan* are both situation comedies, they do not present the same political point of view. The other issue with the methodology is that no one has defined diversity. This particularly becomes an issue when examining the full palette of programming available for the majority of viewers, that is, viewers who get cable or DBS, which represents more than 80% of the country. For instance, if you have a Spanish language channel on cable, is that in and of itself diverse? Much of the programming is similar to formats on English-language channels, so that may not be so. What about something like the Golf Channel? It is simply 24 hr of sports, a format that has existed since the Wednesday Night Fights in the 1950s. Determining a more refined scale and creating an agreed upon definition of diversity is critical to any future research.

Beyond measuring diversity, changes in the economic environment suggest that diversity will continue to decline. The television marketplace has become more complex. Networks are faced with fewer opportunities for syndication both here and abroad; they have become more dependent on reality programming for which there may not be a syndication market; competition for advertising dollars from television, print, and the Internet is increasing, and the networks are part of complex, vertically integrated corporations that must respond to evermore demanding shareholders. If the historical trend continues, increased pressure for increased profit will lead to less risk taking, and thus less diverse programming, on the part of the networks.

We must also keep in mind that diversity is a political issue that has become increasingly contentious in recent times. The June 2, 2003, decision to increase the television ownership caps from 35% of the country to 45% is indicative of just how controversial this issue is. Although the Federal Communications Commission thought it had a rubber stamp to change the ownership caps, citizen groups and Congress told them otherwise. If nothing else, the June 2 decision has brought to the fore the need to seriously debate diversity—what it is, why we want it, and how to achieve it. I suggest that we have an opportunity available in the digital spectrum to create a space where advertising is not the underlying revenue source. Although this may not guarantee diversity, it would guarantee producers a chance to create programming free of consumer constraints.

REFERENCES

Amendment of Part 73 of the Commission's Rules and Regulations with Respect to Competition and Responsibility in Network Television Broadcasting, Report and Order, 23 FCC 2d 382 ("1970 Report and Order").

Amendment of Part 73 of the Commission's Rules with Respect to Competition and Responsibility in Network Television Broadcasting. Notice of Proposed Rule Making, 45 FCC 2146 (1965).

Beebe, J. H. (1977). Institutional structure and program choices in television markets. *The Quarterly Journal of Economics, 91*(1), 15–37.

Chan-Olmsted, S. M. (1996) From Sesame Street to Wall Street: An analysis of market competition in commercial children's television. *Journal of Broadcasting & Electronic Media, 40*(1), 30.

Curran, J. (1991). Mass media and democracy: A reappraisal. In J. Curran & M. Gurevitch (Eds.), *Mass media and society* (pp. 82–117). London: Edward Arnold.

De Jong, A. S., & Bates, B. J. (1991). Channel diversity in cable television. *Journal of Broadcasting & Electronic Media, 35,* 159–166.

Dimmick, J., & McDonald, D. G. (2001). Network radio oligopoly, 1926–1956: Rivalrous imitation and program diversity. *Journal of Media Economics, 14*(4), 197–212.

Dominick, J. R., & Pearce, M. C. (1976). Trends in network prime-time programming, 1953–74. *Journal of Communication, 26,* 70–80.

Einstein, M. (2004). *Media diversity: Economics, ownership and the FCC.* Mahwah, NJ: Lawrence Erlbaum Associates, Inc.

Entman, R. M., & Wildman, S. S. (1992). Reconciling economic and non-economic perspectives on media policy: Transcending the "marketing place of ideas." *Journal of Communication, 42*(1), 5–19.

Grant, A. E. (1994). The promise fulfilled? An empirical analysis of program diversity on television. *Journal of Media Economics, 7*(1), 51–64.

Greco, A. N. (1999). The impact of horizontal mergers and acquisitions on corporate concentration in the U.S. book publishing industry: 1989–1994. *Journal of Media Economics, 12,* 165.

Herskovitz, M. L. (1997). The repeal of the financial interest and syndication rules: The demise of program diversity and television network competition? *Cardozo Arts & Entertainment Law Journal, 15*(1), 177–212.

Le Duc, D. R. (1982). Deregulation and the dream of diversity. *Journal of Communication, 32*(4), 164–178.

Levin, H. J. (1971). Program duplication, diversity, and effective viewer choices: Some empirical findings. *The American Economic Review, 61,* 81–88.

Levine, J., & Fass, A. (2003, March 17). Sex, money and videotape. *Forbes,* 88.

Li, S. S., & Chiang, C. (2001). Market competition and programming diversity: A study on the TV market in Taiwan. *Journal of Media Economics, 14*(2), 105–119.

Litman, B. R. (1979). The television networks, competition and program diversity. *Journal of Broadcasting, 23*(4), 393–409.

McCarthy, M. (2003, May 22). *USA Today.* Retrieved August 14, 2002 from the World Wide Web: www.usatoday.com/money/advertising/2003-05-22-upfront_x.htm

McNeil, A. (1996). *Total television: The comprehensive guide to programming from 1948 to the present* (4th ed.). New York: Penguin.

Media Dynamics (1998). *TV dimensions '98.* New York: Author.

Napoli, P. M. (1999). Deconstructing the diversity principle. *Journal of Communication, 49*(4), 7–34.

Owen, B. M. (1978). The economic view of programming. *Journal of Communication, 28,* 43–50.

Park, S. K. (1999). Trends in the supply of television programs for network and syndication markets. *Feedback, 40*(2), 14–21.

PricewaterhouseCoopers (2000). *Global entertainment and media outlook: 2000–2004.* New York: Author.

Steiner, G. A. (1963). *The people look at television: A study of audience attitudes.* New York: Knopf.

Sterling, C. H., & Kittross, J. M. (1978). *Stay tuned: A concise history of American broadcasting.* Belmont, CA: Wadsworth.

van Cuilenburg, J. (1999). Between media monopoly and ruinous media competition. In Y. N. Zassoursky & E. Vartanova (Eds.), *Media, communications and the open society* (pp. 40–61). Moscow: Faculty of Journalism/IKAR.

van der Wurff, R., & van Cuilenburg, J. (2001). Impact of moderate and ruinous competition on diversity: The Dutch television market. *Journal of Media Economics, 14*(4), 213–229.

Webster, J. G., & Phalen, P. F. (1994). Victim, consumer of commodity? Audience models in communication policy. In J. S. Ettema & D. C. Whitney (Eds.), *Audiencemaking: How the media create the audience* (pp. 19–37). Thousand Oaks, CA: Sage.

Wildman, S. S., & Robinson, K. S. (1995). Network programming and off-network syndication profits: Strategic links and implications for television policy. *Journal of Media Economics, 8*(2), 27–48.

Wober, J. M. (1989). The U.K.: The constancy of audience behavior. In L. B. Becker & K. Schoenbach (Eds.), *Audience responses to media diversification: Coping with plenty* (pp. 91–108). Hillsdale, NJ: Lawrence Erlbaum Associates, Inc.